THE MANY FACES OF SHAME

JO NAUGHTON

Grosvenor House
Publishing Limited

This book is published by
Grosvenor House Publishing Ltd
Link House
140 The Broadway, Tolworth, Surrey, KT6 7HT.
www.grosvenorhousepublishing.co.uk

A CIP record for this book
is available from the British Library

ISBN 978-1-78623-569-5

Some names and details have been changed to protect the
identity of the people whose stories are included in this book.
Bible references are from the New King James version unless
otherwise stated. The Message is also used to help reveal
the heart of certain passages.

This book is dedicated to my dear mum. Your love for the Lord, your tenacity through terrible trials, and your persistent, faith-filled prayers are an inspiration to me and many others.

Acknowledgements

My husband, Paul: Thank you for loving me just as I am and for helping me to become my best.

Prophet Cathy: Thank you for believing in me and encouraging me every step of the way.

Tim Collins: Thank you for investing your wisdom, time and talents in this book.

Freisa Davila: Thank you for lending your creative genius to this book and this ministry.

Healed for Life Team: Thank you for your servant hearts, your lavish love, and your unswerving faith. Thank you for sowing your very lives into this ministry that others may enjoy wholeness and freedom.

Those who shared their stories: Thank you for sharing your painful stories that others might find healing and freedom.

Tokie, Ruth, Robert and Wendy: Thank you for investing hours of your time in painstaking proofreading.

Contents

Introduction

The Many Faces Of Shame will take you on a journey to greater peace and freedom. The Holy Spirit will shine His light into your heart as you read and uncover hidden issues that have been holding you back. He will gently but powerfully bring healing, relief and new joy. It is no accident that you have this book in your hand. God is about to begin a brand-new work on the inside that will bring transformation and restoration. I suggest you read while you are alone so that you are free to respond to the work of the Holy Spirit in your heart.

Chapter 1

DIRTY FOOTPRINTS

My first trip to Africa was awful. I had been invited to join dignitaries, influential business people and key pastors on a mission. From the moment I landed, I felt horribly out of place. When we arrived at our lodgings, we were asked to congregate in the lounge. Our host went around the room introducing us one by one. When she reached me, she announced: "This is Pastor Jo. She has issues."

I could not believe what I heard. The blood drained from my face as I tried to maintain my composure. The room was filled with highly successful people who must have wondered what terrible dysfunction could have prompted such a description. In any setting it would have been a dishonoring introduction. Surrounded by intimidating strangers, it felt like a cruel blow. I am not saying I was sorted, but I could not fathom why I was singled out like that. I smiled extremely awkwardly and then said hello to everyone. The conversation moved on. In seven short words, our host publicly pulled me to pieces.

Have you ever been ridiculed at school or at work and made to feel that your best efforts were inadequate? Have you made a mistake in front of others and wished that the ground would swallow you up? Have you been mocked because you didn't get the joke that made all your peers laugh? Have you been put down in front of people whose opinions were important? Have you been assaulted in a way that left you feeling utterly degraded? Have you been smeared by those you trusted? You may have experienced much worse: a home where shame was used as correction; a school where humiliation was deployed as punishment; or a relationship where abuse was used to control you.

Shame's Mark

Picture a place where everyone wears white. Now imagine a man walks in with a paint gun, splattering disgrace in every direction. Shame marks us. It makes us feel smeared. It almost always causes us to want to shrink back and hide. Because it is so painful, we usually try to bury the memory that made us feel that way and pretend that it never happened. Shame is the feeling that arises when something dishonorable, improper, or ridiculous is done to us or by us. It makes us feel disgraced and degraded.

All sorts of experiences can cause shame. Failure, underachievement, public (and private) put-downs, abuse, racial prejudice and poverty are just some of the ways that shame can strike. Irrespective of the cause, the impact can be debilitating. Shame is not satisfied with making us feel small. It seeks to stifle our lives.

A Big Issue

Men and women across the world are held back by all sorts of heart issues. When I speak about difficult topics such as regret or rejection, people are willing to face their pain. However, any time I minister on shame, the resistance in the room is palpable. It takes time for people to let down their guard and allow God in. There is something so unpleasant about shame that we would rather deny its impact on our lives than acknowledge it is lurking inside. We turn away so often that we have no idea that it is simmering beneath the surface. In truth, it is a universal issue.

I struggled for a long time to choose a title for this book. The obvious - of course - would have been 'Shame'. However, I knew that if I named the book that, no one would even want to pick it up. The vast majority of people are impacted by shame in some way and yet most of us struggle to acknowledge (even to ourselves) that we are affected. That merely amplifies shame's power and we end up cowering as we go through life. That is one of the reasons why I believe this book is vital for every believer who wants to fulfill their purpose.

My Small Start

Shame can be subtle; I have seen its dirty footprint in unexpected areas of my life.

A few years ago, I sought the Lord about how to get this vital healing message out to the masses. I longed for a big breakthrough. Television has always been on my heart so I was sure that that was the answer. I had already appeared on several smaller shows so I believed a big door would open soon. As I prayed, I sensed the Holy Spirit ask me, "What do you have in your hand?" I paused for a moment. This was not what I was expecting to hear. The Holy Spirit prompted me to start ministering via social media. He was asking me to start small. I set a launch date and began my weekly 'broadcasts'.

I believed momentum would build fast so that we could bring healing to the nations. The first few weeks reached good numbers then average viewing leveled off. Of course, I was grateful for the privilege of ministering to the few who tuned in. However, I started to feel embarrassed about the low numbers of people I was reaching. I was believing for thousands but usually reaching hundreds. I knew I had heard God and so I continued. At first, I made sure I announced these appearances. Soon, I preferred not to draw unnecessary attention to myself. I felt stupid because not many people were watching. I was faithful, but I felt ashamed about my small start.

Shrinking Back

You could be embarrassed about the painfully slow growth of your business. Perhaps the people around you have prospered while you have struggled. Their big breakthroughs may make you feel horribly small. Even our dreams can mock us. We look at what we were believing to achieve in the light of the little we have actually accomplished. We may hide our slow progress from others. But it does not stop there. We turn away ourselves because our feeble achievements make us feel like a failure. All too often, we lower our future expectations to avoid further disappointment. Shame always has an aim. It wants you to hang back or hide. Very often, shame is most excruciating when it surrounds a project that is at the heart of your purpose.

Maybe you feel like a fool because your ministry is minuscule or your service in God's house seems unimportant. At Christian conferences, you may dodge the inevitable questions about your role or the size of your congregation. I imagine that you have perfected answers that protect you from revealing the somewhat humiliating truth. You are not alone. Countless others feel exactly the same way.

Heaven's Perspective

God has a different view. Zechariah 4:10 (NLT) says, "Do not despise these small beginnings, for the Lord rejoices to see the work begin..." Scripture instructs us not to despise small starts. When we despise something, we turn away or recoil. It often produces a sense of disgust. When we believe our best efforts are insignificant, it can make us withdraw. Remember, shame always has an aim. It wants you to shrink back and hide. Shame is an enemy that seeks to delay or derail your destiny by getting you to give up, even if it is just for a while.

Starting small is often God's plan. It allows the Lord to work on our hearts so that we are ready to seize opportunity when it knocks. You may have heard the story of how the leader of one of the biggest churches in the world started off. Pastor Cho in South Korea preached to just five people every Sunday for five years. I'm certain that satan tried to cause him to recoil. Thank God that pastor persevered. Hebrews 10:39 reminds us not to recoil: "But we are not of those who draw back..."

Returning to my social media situation... I remember the moment I realized that embarrassment was muting me. Shame about my small start made me try to hide. Shame about the low numbers that tuned in prevented me from pushing onwards in prayer. Shame made me hide and even caused me to lower my expectations. You see, this foul enemy not only uses catastrophic experiences like abuse or public humiliation to derail our destinies. Shame creeps into a whole host of other, apparently unimportant, areas of our lives to try to stifle our progress.

Mocking Whispers

I knew I had to deal with it. I spoke back to the mocking whispers in my mind: "I might not be where I want to be, but I'm not where I used to be either. Every precious person who is impacted by these broadcasts is a great reason to keep going." I shoved shame out of my life and went back to believing in the importance of these weekly messages. Shame had subdued my actions without my knowledge. That's how our foe operates.

If you realize that you are ashamed of small beginnings in any way, God wants to heal your heart and set you free. It does not matter what is causing you to crumple on the inside. I encourage you to get back up. Perhaps you are embarrassed by your job, or your job title. Maybe you are ashamed about your lowly home or the rough neighborhood in which you live. You could be uncomfortable about your education, or lack of qualifications. You may feel that you don't measure up to others' expectations. There are a multitude of reasons why you and I can feel like a fool. However, we should never accept the devil's lies.

The Way Out

God does not want us to learn how to cope. He does not give us strategies for handling our hurts. The Lord does not try to talk us out of every sense of degradation. He wants to remove each mark and erase every foul stain. He longs to take every trace of shame away and bring us to the place where we know that we are brand new.

Shame starts to lose its grip in our lives when it is brought into the light. Ephesians 5:13 (AMPC) says, "But when anything is exposed and reproved by the light, it is made visible and clear; and where everything is visible and clear there is light." Let me explain. Shame's power is often strongest in the shadows. It wants you and I to hide and look away from its pain. Shame is one of the most difficult emotions to articulate because owning these feelings can be excruciating.

It is one thing to say, "How dare my manager speak to me like that?" It requires a lot more courage to admit to yourself, "My boss's public put-down squashed me." Both statements might be true. However, the first denies the pain. When we react that way, we are not acknowledging the real damage that has been done. We may dust ourselves off afterwards and carry on. However, we will probably try to avoid a situation like that arising again. It may cause us to pull back in meetings or keep our views to ourselves. As a result, hidden unhealed hurts dictate our decisions.

Romans 8:14 tells us that the sons of God are supposed to be led by the Spirit of God, not past pain.

Outing Shame

Admitting that we have been hurt and humiliated is the beginning of our healing. God is always looking for honesty. Psalm 51:6 says, "You desire truth in the inward parts..." The Lord longs for us to be real. He is the God of Truth. One of the names of the Holy Spirit is the Spirit of Truth. Jesus is the way, the truth and the life. Truth is the birthplace of transformation. I have often seen people appear embarrassed by the suggestion that they need healing. This is ridiculous. Man is born to trouble (Job 5:7). Life hurts. Buried pain is hiding in the vast majority of people's hearts. Although it can be hard to acknowledge that we feel degraded, it is the brave first step.

Once we have owned our feelings, we need to bring them to God in prayer. Isaiah 9:6 tells us that Jesus is our Wonderful Counselor. The primary role of a counselor is to listen while their client shares their experiences. If offloading to a mere mortal can be therapeutic, imagine how healing it is when we pour out our pain in God's presence. As we describe what we have gone through - in as much detail as possible - we release trapped sadness. As we tell our Heavenly Father how we felt, we get rid of our distress. 1 Peter 5:7 in the Amplified says, "Casting all your cares (all your anxieties, all your worries, and all your concerns, once and for all) on Him, for He cares about you (with deepest affection, and watches over you very carefully)."

Hurl Every Hurt

When we cast a stone, we throw it far away. Casting is neither passive nor effortless. It is deliberately thrusting something. God wants us to hurl every hurt at Him by pouring out the contents of our hearts in His presence. When we pour out our hearts to a trusted friend, we share our deepest and most private thoughts. That is what God wants us to do before Him. As we express ourselves in prayer, we release the pain associated with demeaning experiences. While you offload, you will become increasingly aware of His attentive affection. You will encounter His tender loving care. The very process of heavenly counseling is healing.

Face It

We all get let down, put down, disappointed and dismissed. We all (even occasionally) fall or fail. Everyday experiences can produce pain and - many times - shame. In truth, most of us have emotional baggage buried inside that adversely affects our attitudes and choices. I believe it is better to assume that you may need healing than to shut down and conclude that you are sorted. If you feel sure you are fine, it will take great strength to deliberately place yourself under the spotlight of the Holy Spirit. You will need to be willing to face uncomfortable incidents from . your past. However, I assure you that it will be richly rewarding.

Join The Journey

I invite you to begin a journey. It is a journey to phenomenal freedom. Each chapter of this book deals with a different face of shame. It will be important to surrender afresh to the Holy Spirit. Your heart is deep and complex. It has a myriad of hiding places where old, unwanted emotions are locked away. Don't be surprised when you find yourself taken back to long forgotten memories. Proverbs 20:27 says, "The spirit of a man is the lamp of the Lord, searching all the inner depths of his heart." Please allow Him to shine His light into the depths of your heart while you read. He will uncover hidden hurt that has been hindering your life. The Holy Spirit will seek out buried distress that has been hampering your relationships. He will bring back experiences that are long forgotten and you will probably feel some of the sadness from your past. When you pour it out in His presence, not only will the pain drain away, but a weight will lift off your shoulders. You will know a lightness like never before.

Shame is like a foul shawl that shrouds our dignity. As He heals our heart of its pain, that cloak is stripped away. The stigma that satan tried to pin on you slides off. The Lord will then re-fill you with His wonderfully affirming love. Listen to the way that He wants to re-cover you: "...He has clothed me with garments of salvation, He has wrapped me with a robe of righteousness, as a bridegroom decks himself with a garland, and as a bride adorns herself with her jewels." (Isaiah 61:10 NASB). Picture yourself being re-clothed with His honor and wrapped in His great love. The more we allow the Lord to heal every buried hurt, the more we can become free to fulfill every part of our God-given purpose. Let's pray.

Heavenly Father,

I ask You to start a new work in my life. Shine Your light into the depths of my heart and reveal any hidden hurts that have been holding me back. I open up afresh to You today and ask You to have Your way. As I read each chapter, uncover pain that has been causing me to shrink back or hide. I ask You to take me on a wonderful new journey to peace and freedom.

If you realize that you are carrying any shame as a result of small beginnings, I would love to lead you in prayer now:

Lord, I am embarrassed about my painfully slow start. Lack of progress has made me feel like a failure. I feel stupid and I feel small. It is awful, Lord. (Now tell the Lord in as much detail as possible what you have felt embarrassed about). Please take away all my pain and cleanse me of all shame. Heal my heart, oh Lord, I pray.

Thank You Lord that You delight to see the work begin. Thank You Lord that You rejoice in my obedience. I silence every mocking voice inside my mind and choose to arise again in faith. Thank You that You will complete the wonderful work that You began in me. Many before me started small and many after me will also. I am grateful that You counted me faithful to do Your will. It is an honor and a privilege.

I give You all the praise and glory.

In Jesus' name,

Amen.

Chapter 2

FAILURE

Failing feels awful. It is like a punch in the guts that leaves you reeling. It can rock your confidence and make you angry with yourself and others. I have failed more times than I would like to remember. I have bungled exams, lost jobs, ruined relationships and pastored badly. At a more personal level, I have failed God, messed up in marriage, made mistakes with my children and let down dear friends. Every time I fail it hurts. Even when the issue is unimportant it still stings.

Towards the end of his reign, King David suffered a heartbreaking betrayal. His son Absalom led a revolt against him for the leadership of the nation. David's army arose and they squashed the rebellion. However, the day was more bitter than sweet for David because his son was killed. The king did not want anyone to celebrate. As a result, victorious soldiers who had risked their lives skulked home from the frontline. 2 Samuel 19:3 says, "And the people stole back into the city that day, as people who are ashamed steal away when they flee in battle."

This verse reveals the indignity of feeling like a failure. For a soldier, conquest is everything. They are taught to advance and fight. Fleeing from the frontline is an admission of defeat. The Amplified version of 2 Samuel 19:3 says, "The people slipped into the city stealthily that day as humiliated people steal away when they flee in battle." Failure makes us wants to slip out of the spotlight and hide. It can be horribly humiliating. The shame of failure makes us want to retreat. That is the enemy's plan. He wants to use the embarrassment of failing to make you hide. The devil uses our mess-ups to whisper in our ears: "You don't deserve your destiny. You're no longer up to the task. It's time to throw in the towel." These are lies. Proverbs 24:16 says, "For a righteous man may fall seven times and rise again..." Even the righteous fall. The key is staring failure in the face and getting back up.

Failing At The Fundamentals

There are a number of basic roles and responsibilities that we may take for granted. Marrying, lovemaking, procreating, fathering, mothering and providing - to name just a few. The inability to carry out any one of these functions can deeply affect our self-esteem. Because we all assume that we will waltz through life without any problems, when we hit a wall in one of these areas it can make us feel like a prize failure.

Unmarried

Maybe you imagined that you would be married by the time you reached your twenties. You are now in a very different season and still single. Everywhere you look, friends and family are getting on with their apparently fairy-tale lives while you feel left in the wings. Efforts to set you up or insensitive comments by close companions only make things worse. On the other hand, maybe you feel as though no one notices so you suffer in silence. It is not just the pain of loneliness that can make it unbearable, but also the sense of having failed in one of life's fundamental functions. God wants to take the pain away so that you can be free to believe again.

No Sex In Marriage

I have ministered to many men and women who struggle with sex in marriage. Too many precious people freeze when they are expected to be intimate. Maybe you found out that you cannot handle being touched by your partner. You could clam up when your mate tries to caress you. Or perhaps you lack sexual drive. Not only does this make us feel like a failure but it causes great sadness to our spouses. I understand this issue from bitter personal experience. For eleven years, I struggled in the area of intimacy. I loved my husband with all my heart but I could not handle his touch. I would reject him with such frequency that most men would probably have walked away. It was horribly hurtful for him and awful for me.

For more than a decade of marriage, this caused almost constant distress. At the start, I really believed that my husband was the one at fault. I could not understand why a spiritual man was so consumed with sex! I was convinced that once a month should be enough. Thankfully, I wanted to be a mother, so that kept me going for a season. However, when that period passed, the problem grew. After about five years of denial, I began to realize that I was the one with a problem. Deep down inside, I believed that intercourse was unclean and that my body was dirty. Whenever my husband reached out to me, I would push him away.

Until The Healing Begins

Then my healing journey started. The Holy Spirit shone His light into the depths of my heart and revealed buried self-hatred. I disliked myself to such an extent that I had rejected my own body. As God healed me, I began to unfurl. Eager to see me completely free, my husband asked me to study the story of Peter on the rooftop. In Acts 10:15 God spoke to the apostle and said,

"Do not call anything impure that God has made clean." (NIV). Meditating on that verse, the truth began to change my mindset. I realized that I had believed that both my body and matrimonial intimacy were unclean. The truth of God's word began to change me from the inside and then I was delivered from an unclean spirit. After eleven years of agony, I was finally free.

If you find it difficult to be intimate with your spouse, the Lord wants to heal your heart and your marriage. Please don't settle for a sexless relationship. It is not good for you and it is not fair on your partner. Just as Jesus paid the price for our physical and mental health, He also made the way for matrimonial happiness. 1 Corinthians 7:3 (NLT) says, "The husband should fulfill his wife's sexual needs, and the wife should fulfill her husband's needs..." This makes it clear that holding back is not the biblical option. Please make the decision to stay on your healing journey until you are completely free. I have had the privilege of leading many to freedom at our two day Healed for Life conferences. What He will do for one, He will do for us all. As you allow the Lord to take away the shame, you will be able to rise strong and believe for your breakthrough.

Divorce

Many years ago I heard a minister say, "I think the church has made divorce the second unforgivable sin." I don't think that is the case anymore. However, for some the shame of divorce can be shattering. Perhaps you feel cast away, as though you were chewed up and spat out. You could feel like soiled goods. Someone tried you out and then dropped you for a newer model. Maybe you feel as though you failed in the single most important relationship in your life. You may try to avoid mentioning your marital status, or your past. God does not want any amount of shame to stick. The blood of Jesus has the power to deal with every shred of shame, even when it runs very deep.

Being Barren or Firing Blanks

Marriage is demanding. Hannah (whose story is told in 1 Samuel 1) had the added difficulty of sharing her husband with another woman. From the beginning of time, God intended marriage to be a union between one man and one woman. Whenever the original plan is perverted, it causes pain to precious people. Hannah and her rival Peninnah will both have felt the rejection and shame of sharing a husband. If you have suffered the hurt of infidelity, you will understand something of their suffering. We will look at this very painful process further on in this chapter.

Hannah had another agonizing issue. Her dream was to be a mother. She longed to carry a child and watch him grow. The desire was strong. When we feel as though we have failed to fulfill one of our basic functions, it can produce an awful sense of worthlessness. Hannah will have felt that she was unable to perform one of her duties as a wife and a woman. Hannah was barren. This must have made her feel like a failure. To add insult to injury, Peninnah gloated over Hannah's fruitless life with cruel comments and regular ridicule. I will come back to Hannah at the end of this chapter.

Perhaps that's your heartache. You are longing to have children but nothing is happening. Maybe tests have suggested that it is highly unlikely or even impossible. It is not just the disappointment that can hurt so much. There could be the added agony of feeling like you have failed in one of your roles in life. Shame always makes us want to hide. Sometimes we hide from the facts and go into denial. It is too uncomfortable to admit how we really feel so we say something else instead. God is able to give you your heart's desire. However, you will probably need to be full of faith. According to Romans 10:10, faith lives and grows in our hearts. It will be hard for your heart to be full of faith if you are shrouded by shame. Let me repeat what I have said several times already. Shame thrives in the shadows. It starts to lose its power when it is brought into the light. We are going to deal with all these issues in prayer at the end of this chapter. For now, please start to acknowledge any area where you are weighed down.

"I'm A Terrible Parent!"

When children are young, it is easy to get swept along by the busyness of life. Days merge into weeks and weeks into months. Much of the time, parents firefight their way through their children's early years and into adolescence. By the time you are able to lift your head above the fray, the majority of parenting mistakes have already been made. Even if you did your best to get it right, you will no doubt have also got it wrong. What makes matters worse is that you may feel that any flaws you see in your children are the result of your failure. Far too many parents feel like they have failed in the single most important job of their lives: raising their children.

Occasionally, a child grows up in excellent shape, serving God and making great decisions. All too often, that is not the case. Parents feel sad and ashamed, wishing they could wind back the clock and put right their wrongs. Perhaps financial pressure meant you could not provide for them in the way that you had wished. Maybe marital problems took their toll and you know your children were denied the stable home they deserved. The sense of disappointment can be devastating.

Raising A Murderer

Let's look at scripture to put parenting into context. The Bible's first mother and father raised a murderer: Cain. Isaac disliked one of his sons. Rebekah probably neglected Esau. Jacob showed favoritism. Judah's eldest sons were so evil that they died.

Neither Eli the Priest nor Prophet Samuel could control his boys. Jesse forgot about David, David didn't discipline Amnon, and Solomon probably didn't even know all his children! What is my point? Parenting is difficult and even some of the best got it horribly wrong.

Now let's look at this from the children's perspective. Despite a distant dad and a somewhat manipulative mum, Jacob fulfilled his destiny and became Israel. Joseph became one of the Old Testament's finest leaders even though he grew up without his mother. Even though he did not have an affirming father, David became Israel's greatest king. Even though her mum and dad died when she was young, Esther became queen and was used to save her nation. So what's my point this time? God is bigger than our blunders and He is able to make up for our mistakes. Our children need our persistent prayers. While you feel like you've failed, it will be hard to have faith for their breakthrough.

Lay It Down

If you have been carrying this burden, I want to encourage you to lay it down. Part of the problem with shame is that we often avoid admitting the truth because it is intensely uncomfortable. However, the weight that we carry is the very burden that we try to deny. I encourage you to face every sense of failure that has built up inside. The rewards of handing them over are truly wonderful.

About a year ago, my daughter had an accident. At the time, I was in America ministering. My husband Paul called me to let me know that Abby had fallen off her bike and hurt her wrist. I was due to fly home the following evening so although I was upset to be so far away, I reassured myself that I would be home soon. I arrived back two days later. Once safely home, my husband called me and asked if I was sitting down. Paul had very thoughtfully withheld the full facts to protect me. Now that I was back, he told me exactly what had happened...

Abby had been cycling downhill in the woods at about 25 miles per hour when she must have hit a rock. She was thrown off her bicycle. An ambulance reached the scene about the same time my husband arrived. Covered in blood, Abby was rushed to the emergency room. She had broken her jaw in two places and needed multiple stitches all over her face. And yes, she also fractured her wrist. I will never forget the moment that my husband brought my daughter home from the hospital. Paul brought Abby into our living room where I was sitting. However hard I searched, I could not see my little girl. Abby's face was so swollen and disfigured that she was unrecognizable. She could only see out of a tiny slit in one eye. I sat with her on the sofa for hours.

I Wasn't There For You

Apart from the agony of seeing my daughter in so much pain, one other issue was eating away at me. I was not there when Abby needed me the most. I could not imagine how frightened she must have felt. Girls need their mothers, especially when things go wrong. But I was thousands of miles away. My amazing husband had to handle the whole trauma alone. I felt terrible but I was struggling to even acknowledge the guilt and feelings of failure. Later that day, I got into God's presence and forced the brutal truth out of my mouth: "Father, I wasn't there. My little girl needed me and I was not there for her." I told the Lord that I felt like I had failed both my daughter and my husband. After all, he was forced to be mom and dad. I wept while God healed my heart.

Let me stop there for a moment. Very often, the reason we get weighed down is that we can't bring ourselves to say the one thing that is heaviest on our hearts. Shame always tries to hide. However, while it is hidden, we will be weighed down. My family had been traumatized and I needed to be strong. The only way that you and I can be our best when it matters most is if we deal with hidden heart issues. Ephesians 5:13 says that anything that is exposed to the light becomes light. When a fear or a regret is hidden in our hearts, it has the power to pull us down. Once we bring it into the light, it loses its grip.

What is the buried sadness of your soul? What are the regrets or feelings of failure hiding in your heart? You can say it all in God's presence. You can tell Him what you couldn't tell anyone else.

God's Got Them

When I came out of my prayer closet, I sat again with my daughter. Although it was difficult, I now had the courage to say what I couldn't admit before: "Abby, I am so sorry that I was not there when you needed me most." My big deal might sound like nothing to you but it was a mountain to me. I was peering through a tiny crack in my daughter's eye. Although she couldn't speak or eat, she somehow managed to reply, "I didn't need you, Mummy. Daddy was amazing." My husband also told me they managed fine without me. I was blown away. To be honest, I was ready for anything because of God's healing balm in prayer, but her response and his reassurance refreshed my soul. We don't often get that kind of human closure. However, we can always get a heavenly perspective. It demands the kind of honesty referenced in Psalm 51:6: "Behold, You desire truth in the inner being..." (Amplified). When we pour out the pain of our apparent failure, whatever that might be, He will heal our hearts. Once every weight has been taken away, we can arise strong in faith and believe again for our children's well-being.

Cheating

Infidelity is agony. It is heartbreaking for everyone affected. Very often, this fragile area of shattered trust leads to separation and divorce. If you have suffered as a result of unfaithfulness, God wants to heal your heart. I encourage you to read my books *Lifting the Mask* and *My Whole Heart.* Allow the Lord to reach into the depths of your soul and take your pain away. At the same time, if you were the one who was unfaithful, our Heavenly Father wants to restore you too. The enemy will try to use the guilt and shame to keep you bound to the past. Our God is able to bring total transformation.

Clive and Sue were pastors of the church they inherited from Clive's father. Their three children were aged twelve, nine and three years when Clive fell into sin with a young woman who had been serving in their ministry. It was a Monday morning when Clive told his wife (and his leaders) about the affair. Sue was stunned. As the reality of the situation sunk in, shame covered her like a cloak. Sue reflected, "I felt like a complete failure, like I was pushed aside because I wasn't a good enough wife. It was humiliating. As time passed, I felt awful when I saw people from my church. This just made me feel even worse. I wanted to run away."

For Clive, the sense of failure crashed around him. He explained, "I failed God, I failed my dad who planted the church, I failed my wife, I failed my children, and I failed our congregation. My mistakes tore many people's lives apart. As a pastor, my phone rang off the hook and a constant barrage of emails filled my inbox. After I fell, the silence was deafening. People who saw me in the street either looked away or asking prying questions. My failure was public, and everyone had an opinion. I was unbearably ashamed of myself."

With help from an incredibly supportive pastor, Clive and Sue were helped on a journey of restoration. Clive prioritized his family and Sue forgave. But the shame tried to stick. Sue came to Healed for Life several years later. It was there that God set her free. Every memory was transformed from a source of scorn to a tool to help others. The couple found a new church. Soon after joining, Clive told his story to one of the associate pastors. Far from the judgment he feared, the pastor welcomed him with open arms and said, "We are so glad that you have joined us. This is a place of restoration." His response helped seal Clive's new season. Now Clive and Sue are part of the marriage and family ministry in their church, helping bringing restoration to others.

I Can't Provide

There is something built into the heart of a parent that creates a desire to provide. When work dries up or circumstances squeeze, it can be deeply degrading. It can make a person feel like they are failing, or even worse, like a failure. Perhaps you had hopes for a better life that appear to have come to nothing. It might make you feel like a fraud. However, it is too hard to admit, so instead you express anger at your circumstances. Perhaps you pretend that life is good. All the while, shame eats away at you on the inside.

During a major drought in Israel's history, a sparse harvest made some farmers feel too embarrassed to lift up their heads. The drought was not their doing, yet their inability to provide made them feel degraded: "Because the ground is parched, for there was no rain in the land, the plowmen were ashamed; they covered their heads." (Jeremiah 14:4). Their failure was not their fault, but this did not lessen their sense of disgrace. When we cover our heads, look down to the ground or gaze the other way, we are trying to avoid being seen by people. Have you ever wished the ground would swallow you up? Have you ever wanted to crawl away from a situation? Shame is foul and its effects are vicious.

Money Speaks

Virtually everything has a price tag. Food, fashion, furniture and family vacations all come at a cost. Even time, as they say, is money. More often than not, the price of an item determines its value. Summing up the world's system, Ecclesiastes 10:19b says, "...money answers everything." This has consequences. If you are handsomely rewarded for your work, it will probably enhance your view of your value. Sadly, the opposite is also true. If you are poorly paid or without work, it may make you feel inferior. You have probably heard people say, "If you pay peanuts, you get monkeys." Such sentiments can make us feel worthless when we are not properly rewarded for our best efforts. If despite every effort, we struggle to find work, it can make us feel cheap. If this is you, it may have altered your view of your value.

God wants to take away that pain and strip away any shame. His view of your value is immense. Deuteronomy 7:6b says, "...Of all the people on earth, the Lord your God has chosen you to be his own special treasure." (NLT) Segulâ is the Hebrew word for special treasure. It means jewel or highly valued property. That is your Heavenly Father's estimation of your great worth.

It's Not Enough

In our social media society, we are constantly bombarded by images of everyone else's dazzling successes. In the light of our friends' glittering testimonies, it is easy to feel like a flop. There are times that I have opened Facebook in an upbeat mood. However, I might go back to work discouraged. The achievements of others can make our status quo seem horribly substandard. We can end up being embarrassed about our own progress. That may cause us to want to quit or at least slow down. That is why we must always deal with every shred of shame.

Underachievement can erode your sense of dignity. It can make you feel less valuable than those who are successful. It can produce a sense of inadequacy. Often, the longer we feel like we are underachieving, the greater the damage. The problem can then be compounded. According to Proverbs 23:7, your view of yourself affects how your life turns out: "... as a man thinks in his heart so is he..." This means that the more I look down upon myself, the more I limit my chances of breaking out of negative cycles. It is all too common for God's precious people to see themselves as insufficient or inadequate. We then continue to fulfill our own low expectations and get trapped in a rut. We need to face every feeling of failure so that God can turn our lives around.

Overshadowed

Do you feel overshadowed? It may be that one prominent person makes you feel like a failure. Alternatively, you might constantly compare yourself with others and deem yourself inferior. They may be more successful, smarter or faster. Perhaps you can't quite work out why you feel so squashed by the success of others. Maybe it just makes you feel small and ashamed of your station in life.

As we have already learned, shame thrives in the shadows. It grows in the dark. When we shine the light of truth into the place of shame, sometimes it is instantly dispelled. There are no two people in the world who are identical. Of the billions of men and women who have lived and died over countless generations, no individual has had the same fingerprints as another. Although so-called identical twins are born across the world, no two people are in fact identical. Their smiles, walk, humor and expressions are different. There are no duplicates and there never will be. You are unique.

It is not just your physical appearance that makes you different. Psalms 33:15 tells us that your soul is unique too: "He fashions their hearts individually..." You and I are unlike anyone else. So why do we spend our lives measuring ourselves against people who are different? When I compare my job, my children, my ministry, my position, my life or my gifts, I may just be straying outside my business. God made me unique so how can I determine my success or failure by comparing myself with others?

Of course, some comparison is perfectly healthy. We rummage through clothes in our favorite shop to find the garment we like the most. We compare prices to find the best deal. However, it is a problem when we compare ourselves with other people. It can be catastrophic when the person making the comparisons has a low opinion of their own value. In that context, if we continue comparing ourselves with other people, we can end up feeling ashamed of ourselves. We may even develop a deep-seated sense of self-hatred.

No Comparison

The Amplified version of 1 Corinthians 15:10 is powerful. It says, "But by the grace (the unmerited favor and blessing) of God I am what I am...". Scripture is saying that you are the way you are by the favor of God. My husband Paul is Irish. Like some of his kinsmen, he has huge hands and big ears. Growing up, he used to despise these features and try to hide himself. He would look at other kids on his street and wish he looked like them. After he got saved, God took him on an amazing healing journey. As part of this process, the verse we just read came alive on the inside. He realized that it was because of God's goodness and favor that he had big hands and ears. Hands to heal and ears to hear the voice of God. The truth can change our perspective.

Dealing With The Shame Of Failure

It is hard to be full of faith for breakthrough when we are ashamed of the status quo. Faith is of the heart so our hearts need to be free to believe. As we saw earlier, our Bible character Hannah modeled the right way to deal with the pain of failure. She withdrew from the world and faced her pain in the presence of God. She opened up in prayer and shared her great sadness. She wept buckets before her Heavenly Father. Afterwards, she explained to Eli the priest, "I am a woman of sorrowful spirit. I... have poured out my soul before the Lord... Out of the abundance of my complaint and grief I have spoken until now." (1 Samuel 1:15-16). She poured out her disappointment and pain in God's presence. She let go of the weight and allowed the Lord to heal her wound.

Because she had released her anguish, Hannah was now free to believe again. She made a faith-filled covenant with God that if He would give her a son, she would dedicate the child to the ministry. God heard her prayer, Eli released a prophetic promise and Hannah gave birth to a baby boy called Samuel. She dedicated Samuel to the Lord and went on to have five more children. After her pain and shame were taken away, Hannah's desire was fulfilled.

What's Your Story?

What are the forgotten failures that have caused your heart to be weighed down? What are the buried regrets that still sting when they cross your consciousness? Trying not to face something does not make it go away. In fact, it often heightens the impact it has on your life. When we feel like we have failed in our most fundamental roles in life, the weight of responsibility can be crushing. If you are carrying the shame of failure, I would love to lead you in prayer the Hannah way.

Heavenly Father,

I feel like a failure. (Now tell the Lord what has been buried in your heart. Is it the pain of singleness, failure in marriage, in intimacy, in parenting, or providing? Do you feel like you are underachieving? Explain exactly what had made you feel like you have failed. Be as honest and specific as possible.) All of this has made me feel ashamed of myself. Father, please reach into the depths of my heart and take my pain away. Help me to tell You whenever I feel ashamed of my performance. Help me to always pour out my pain in Your presence.

Now heal my heart, I pray, Oh Lord. Thank You that You cover my nakedness and thank You that You are bigger than any mistake I have made. I put my trust in You again, Oh Lord. Thank You that as I surrender, You will work it all together for my good. I give You all the praise and glory.

In Jesus' name,

Amen.

Chapter 3

HUMILIATION

Towards the end of a grueling trip, I was scheduled to minister at a small church on the East Coast of America. Even before I arrived, I was exhausted. I had been away for a while, so I was also feeling homesick. As I walked up the path towards the church, I was greeted by a series of blank faces. When you arrive at a church where you are due to minister, you will usually be ushered into a side room to meet the key leaders. No-one seemed to even acknowledge our arrival. I made my way into the auditorium. It was obvious that something was out of turn. Feeling extremely awkward, I took a seat. Soon, the service started. After a few minutes, one of my team called me out of the worship. She nervously explained, "They aren't expecting you. They have another guest speaker booked."

I was bewildered. I stood in the foyer while phone calls were made to try to determine what had happened. I felt like a spare part. Everyone was looking at me and wondering what on earth I was doing there. One of the church elders seemed somewhat suspicious. This just added to the humiliation. I felt like an uninvited guest that had been caught by bouncers trying to get into a party without a ticket. I wished the ground would swallow me up. Eventually, I was summoned into an office and asked to take a seat.

JO NAUGHTON

I Wish I Could Vanish

I was informed that the senior leader who had invited me to minister thought I was no longer available. As a result, he had booked another speaker to take my place. After explaining what had happened, he asked if I would stay and minister at the altar for twenty minutes after the preacher had finished. I was 5,000 miles away from home and I felt like a reject. I wanted to make myself disappear. However, because I know I am supposed to walk in humility and love, I agreed to stay.

I had about an hour to get restored. God still wanted to minister to the hearts of His people. I needed a healed heart and a simple word. As I sat in the pew listening to the preacher, I talked to my Heavenly Father from my heart. "I feel like a complete fool, Lord. Like a spare part. I am embarrassed and lonely. Please heal my heart of all this humiliation." The healing love of the Lord filled my heart and my peace returned. I looked at the leaders in that place. They were dedicated and humble. I asked God to bless them.

After the speaker had finished, the pastor introduced me very graciously. As I took the microphone, the anointing descended. God moved in an amazing way, healing many hurting hearts. He did in twenty minutes what would normally have taken two hours. But here's the point: the humiliation hurt. If I had not been healed, I would probably have left offended. I may have given God a bad name and the purposes of the Lord would have been thwarted. Humiliation is hard to admit because it feels so terrible. We would rather express offence or annoyance. But being honest with ourselves, and with God, paves the way for relief. When we are humiliated, we need to be real and we need to be healed.

Exposed

There is an awful story in the second book of Samuel. King David and the King of Ammon were friends. So when this king died, David wanted to support his grieving son, Hanun. David decided to send some ambassadors to travel to the nearby nation and express his heartfelt sympathy. Unfortunately, Hanun was suspicious of David's motives. He supposed that David's ambassadors were spies sent to overthrow the city. Instead of receiving the gentlemen as guests, Hanun and his staff humiliated them.

We will pick up the story in 2 Samuel 10:4-5 (NLT): "So Hanun seized David's ambassadors and shaved off half of each man's beard, cut off their robes at the buttocks, and sent them back to David in shame. When David heard what had happened, he sent messengers to tell the men, 'Stay at Jericho until your beards grow out, and then come back.' For they felt deep shame because of their appearance."

These leaders were chosen for this sensitive mission because they were honorable and dependable. They left their families at home to serve their king and country. However, instead of being celebrated, they were humiliated. Deeply disgraceful things often happen to really precious people. The experience makes us feel marked. Psalm 44:15 (NLT) expresses the impact: "We can't escape the... humiliation; shame is written across our faces." If you have been humiliated, the enemy will try to tell you that you are a disgrace. It is really important to realize that this is one of shame's foul lies. You are just as honorable now as you were before the enemy uncovered you. The devil should be ashamed, not you.

Men And Women

The Bible is clear that the needs of men and women are different. Scripture instructs husbands to love and wives to submit. Women thrive when strong men are tender. In the same way, a man can be his best when his spouse shows genuine respect. Leadership is challenging. I believe that God asks wives to submit to help husbands with the tricky task of domestic headship. The Lord looks at the heart so when He considers if I am submissive, He will not only consider my behavior. The Lord will look at my heart toward my husband. I believe the best phrase to sum up what God wants a wife to show her man is heart-felt respect.

Heart-felt respect can create an atmosphere for a man to shine. When a woman builds up her husband in public and honors him at home, it helps him thrive. Of course it is easier to respect someone who is behaving well! But the Bible does not say wives should submit if their husbands deserve it. We need to learn to honor headship.

Chipping Away

When a woman constantly undermines her husband, it can chip away at his dignity. It can strip him of his God-given identity and leave him feeling emasculated. If you have felt cut down to size by the words or actions of your wife or another woman, God wants to heal your heart. The Lord wants to reach into your identity and restore you in that place where your dignity has been eroded. He wants you to rise up again, secure and strong. For now, please acknowledge to the Lord that you have felt stripped of your honor. He is here to heal.

Shame in marriage can be destructive. It causes us to hide when we need to communicate. It makes us shut down when we should be opening up. It tries to drive a wedge between a husband and wife. We cover up, we push each other away for fear of being exposed or seen. That is never God's best. The original plan of the Lord is made plain in Genesis 2:25: "And they were both naked, the man and his wife, and were not ashamed." God's purpose was that marriage would be a place of openness and rest.

A union where two people could enjoy one another without any fear or self-consciousness. The devil uses shame to try to divide.

Back to the ambassadors... They were half shaved to look like fools at a time when beards were a sign of manhood. I can imagine the foreign barbers mocking as they sheared off their beards. This callous act will have made these men feel utterly emasculated.

Many years ago, the Lord spoke to me (out of the blue!) about leading men. He said, "Jo, if you are going to start ministering to men, you will have to change the way you treat them." You need to understand that I had no desire back then to minister to males. I thought that was my husband's job! I felt uncomfortable speaking into their lives. This did not seem to bother God. He continued, "You cannot treat men the way you treat women." I understood what He meant immediately. I sometimes give clear instructions to my female leaders. I feel no need to wrap up my directions in cotton wool. God was showing me how to get the best out of my brothers. I needed to make sure that all my requests were framed with extra respect. I now consider ministering to men a joy and an immense privilege.

Undermined

Of course, it is not just your partner that can strip you of your dignity. Perhaps you have been undermined at work or ridiculed at church. Maybe your family are constantly making condescending comments and their words have ground you down. It could be that you have experienced some sort of trauma that has decimated your self-respect. In these circumstances, the enemy wants us to pretend we felt no pain. The devil knows how hard it is to face such uncomfortable emotions so he tempts us to turn away and bury the hurtful feelings. Remember, pain is always better out than in.

The ambassadors' ordeal did not stop there. These grown men were stripped of their clothes - and their dignity. Their tunics were cut at the waist so that their buttocks were exposed for all to see (and sneer). They were sent out of Hanun's palace naked from the waist down. There is something about being exposed that is excruciating. It can make us feel debased and degraded. If you have been exposed through abuse, we are going to deal with this terrible pain in chapter 6. For now, we will look at other forms of exposure. You might not have been stripped literally. However, you may have been treated in ways that made you feel like a complete fool.

Public Put-downs

Susan is a senior executive. She was promoted to Vice President in a strategic organization. The new job was the culmination of years of hard work so she was excited about the new position. Within a couple of weeks of her promotion, Susan was asked to present a short proposal at a meeting of more than forty senior leaders. She had barely finished when her chief executive tore into her and undermined everything she had said. He picked her presentation apart and ridiculed her contributions. Susan was stunned. It felt like a massive public put-down in a room full of old men in suits. She made her way home at the end of the day and tried to process what had happened. The assault was humiliating and brutal, but she picked herself up and carried on.

A few months later, Susan attended one of our healing conferences. At the end of one of the sessions, I spoke about shame at work. The Holy Spirit took her back to the events in the boardroom and she broke down. She had not realized how deeply that experience had battered her self-belief. Susan wept in God's presence as He healed her heart. She left with a fresh determination and a lightness inside. Her confidence was restored.

Cruel Comments

If unkind comments have wounded you, please ask the Lord to heal your heart. Ask your Heavenly Father to take the pain of the words away. Perhaps you were publicly put down in front of co-workers. It could be that your boss did not defend you, or maybe he or she was the one undermining you. All too often, we think work shouldn't hurt and so we try to shrug off any shame. The Bible instructs us to remove sorrow from our hearts in Ecclesiastes 11:10. It does not matter where you were wounded. It matters that you get healed.

Everyone Around May Be Laughing...

Maybe you have been mocked. When one person ridicules another it can be horribly humiliating. It is bad enough in private, but the pain of being the butt of other people's jokes escalates if it is done in public. Everyone around you may be laughing while you shrivel up on the inside. Sometimes oversensitivity to workplace banter is a symptom of public humiliation in childhood. The enemy wants you to feel smeared by your experiences. He does not want you to acknowledge how much you were hurt. It serves his purposes when you refuse to look back. The devil wants to keep every form of shame hidden so that he can secretly torment you whenever he likes. By contrast, God wants to reach into that place of pain and heal your heart. He is ready to roll away every sense of reproach. The Lord wants to bring lasting healing and freedom.

When I was a child, I was close friends with a girl who lived on a small farm. Her family had a huge dog which looked more like a small donkey. One summer's afternoon, I was playing with my friend when her father returned home from work. As he entered the house, I heard him bellow at the top of his voice, "Get out of this house, NOW!" I jumped to my feet and ran as fast as my little legs would carry me. Once safely outside the house, I turned to see the entire family standing on the doorstep laughing. My friend's father had been addressing the dog, not me! I turned a dark shade of crimson, returned to the house and tried to forget the affair. However, far from finding it funny, I felt completely humiliated.

Ridicule can be excruciating for people who already struggle with rejection. If you battle with insecurity, then mockery may be agony. The truth is that scorn does not shake stable people in the same way. However, I was neither secure nor stable as a little girl. I did not really like myself and I assumed other people did not like me either. As a result, this harmless misunderstanding choked me on the inside. I avoided going to that girl's house from that day and we grew apart. Shame always tries to direct our decisions and constrain our lives, even when its entry point is innocent. God healed my heart decades later and drained the buried shame away. Since then, I have had the privilege of leading many at our Healed for Life conferences to be healed of childhood humiliation.

Correction

I am both a pastor and a preacher. In my opinion, being a pastor is far harder! Preachers get to deliver mighty messages to massive crowds and then disappear. Pastors have to stay behind and clean up the mess. When we need to bring correction to a situation in our church, my husband often asks me to be "bad cop". In other words, I bring the painful challenge and he offers comfort afterwards. It is not always that way round but I certainly do my fair share of tricky tasks. I do not enjoy that side of the job, even for a moment. It would be easier to leave people to their own devices. We challenge (hopefully as kindly as possible) for love's sake. Even when correction is kind, it can be difficult to hear. When feedback is handled badly, it can be devastating.

If you have been belittled for your blunders, it can make you believe you will never succeed. It can create a sense of inadequacy. Challenge helps us to grow when it is done the right way. However, cruelty is not God's tool of transformation. Emma was raised by a violent father and a caring but controlling mother. Her dad would lash out at her any time she missed the mark. "You stupid fool," he would yell as he slapped his daughter about the face. Although her mother was calm and collected, she also used shame to try to change Emma's behavior. "You look like an idiot when you bite your nails", or: "You embarrass me when you dress like a mess." Humiliation is not God's rod of correction.

You're Allowed To Make Mistakes!

Maybe you can relate to Emma's experiences. Perhaps you were publicly humiliated in school for getting things wrong. Maybe you were put down by your parents for making a mess. You could have been humiliated at work for simple slip-ups. Every one of us should be allowed to make mistakes. Messing up does not make you a mess. That is what shame will try to make you believe. Proverbs 22:8b says, "...the rod of anger will fail." Anger should not be your teacher, and nor should shame. If you have been wounded by cruel correction, God wants to heal your heart.

One of the problems with passive aggressive personalities is that they can be painfully unpredictable. My father could be subdued for days then suddenly he would snap. All would seem calm, then he would lash out and thrash us. One time, I was severely spanked for not tidying away my shoes. I had left them on the stairs and when I didn't jump to attention the first time he asked, my father erupted. After the beating, I was sent to my room where I cried alone for what felt like hours. My body was sore, but that was nothing compared to the unbearable pain in my heart. I felt ashamed and angry with myself for being so stupid. I was eight.

My crime was not coming running the moment my name was called.

When shame is used to punish, it often makes its victims feel angry and upset with themselves. When you are put down for your mistakes, it can feel like you are being labeled a failure. This does not usually empower people to change. Even if frustration or fear pushes you to perform better for a season, it will not usually lead to lasting improvement. Proverbs 23:7 says, "As a man thinks in his heart, so is he." When authority figures use ridicule or cruelty to correct us, it can batter our self-belief (how we think in our hearts), and therefore who we become.

It is probably impossible to avoid humiliation because life is full of exposing experiences. The key is to make sure you get healed. If the Holy Spirit has highlighted one particular memory, focus on that as we pray. If you realize that you have suffered in many ways, take your time and deal with them one by one. Let's pray.

Heavenly Father,

I realize that I am carrying the pain of being humiliated (Now tell the Lord exactly what happened in as much detail as you can.) I felt so exposed. It was awfully embarrassing. It was horrible, Lord. I felt stripped of my dignity and I was made to feel foolish. Heal my heart, oh Lord, I pray. Take away every sense of feeling stupid. Reach into my heart and heal me where it hurt.

Thank You, Lord, that You always protect me. Thank You, Lord, that You cover me with Your dignity. I receive Your love afresh. I arise again knowing that I am Your special treasure.

I love You, Lord, and I give You all the glory.

In Jesus' name, I pray,

Amen.

Chapter 4

REJECTION

Steve first fell for Tracy when they were teenagers. All their friends and family knew that Steve would have done anything to win Tracy's heart. However, she never felt the same way. They went on to higher education and lost touch. Steve gave his life to the Lord in his early twenties and got involved in a local church. About a decade later, Tracy was saved and she joined Steve's church. He was blown away and soon found his long-forgotten feelings being rekindled. Within a matter of months, the two were courting. Steve was sure she was the one. Church friends were delighted to see Steve so happy and everyone assumed they would be hearing wedding bells very soon.

After just three months together, Tracy lost interest in Steve. She met someone else and dumped her childhood friend. He was completely heartbroken. He could not believe that he had been so wrong about the girl of his dreams. That was not all. He felt horribly humiliated. Steve felt like a complete fool in front of all of his church family and friends. He had shouted about his undying love from the rooftops. He had told his story of love lost and found to everyone. He was crushed. Rejection is agony enough. But all too often, it also makes us feel degraded. We may acknowledge the pain but bury the shame of desertion. As a result, we get stuck. Steve struggled to get past his heartbreak. He could not understand why the sadness would not leave. When he eventually admitted that he felt a deep sense of disgrace, the pain lost its grip. Healing flowed and Steve embraced life with his head held high.

Not Wanted

We are made to be in a relationship with one another and to live in love and harmony. When we are pushed away, it can wound very deeply. Even Jesus experienced its gut-wrenching pain. Looking ahead to the price He would have to pay, Jesus associated the pain of rejection with the suffering of dying: "The Son of Man must suffer many things, and be rejected by the elders... and be killed..." Luke 9:22. Jesus was rejected by prominent leaders and well respected teachers. He was despised by the very people He came to save.

Rejection can come at us from all sorts of different directions. You may have been pushed away by your parents - in adulthood as well as childhood. When the people who were supposed to adore you dismiss or even despise you, the wounds can run deep. Perhaps you were betrayed by your brother or sister, or even your whole family. It might not have been at home where you were hurt. Perhaps you were shunned by close friends with whom you shared your heart and life. At work, maybe you were belittled by your boss or alienated by your co-workers. Perhaps you have been turned down (over and over again) by potential schools or employers. Whichever way it comes, rejection really hurts. It also tells us a whole host of lies. When we are not wanted, it can make us feel inferior. It can cause us to doubt our value. It can make us believe that we are second best. All these negative assumptions can leave us feeling ashamed of ourselves.

When rejection takes root in our hearts, it is as if we are living life outside a glass window - looking in on everyone else. If you're in that place, you may believe that nothing you do is ever good enough. Deep down inside, you not only feel rejected. You may see yourself as a reject. You might dislike, or even despise, yourself. On eight separate occasions, the Bible says, "Love your neighbor as yourself..." (Leviticus 19:18, Matthew 19:19, Matthew 22:39, Mark 12:31, Luke 10:27, Romans 13:9, Galatians 5:14, James 2:8). It is not alright to reject yourself. We must be healed of the shame of rejection so that we can love ourselves and other people.

The Ugly Duckling

Leah is one of the Bible's leading ladies. She mothered half of Israel's founding leaders: Reuben, Simeon, Levi, Judah, Issachar and Zebulun. Jesus is the Lion of the Tribe of Judah so Leah carried our Savior's seed. She was strategic to God's plan for mankind. Sometimes we assume that if God is going to use us then our life will be a bed of roses. In truth, suffering is sometimes a sign of the purposes of God. Leah had a harrowing journey.

She is first introduced in Genesis 29:16-17 (AMPC): "Now Laban had two daughters; the name of the elder was Leah and the name of the younger was Rachel. Leah's eyes were weak and dull looking, but Rachel was beautiful and attractive." Being compared to other people can be awful. For Leah it must have been unbearable. She had a stunning sister called Rachel. Her little sister was not only beautiful. She was attractive too. I don't even know what that looks like! In contrast, Leah's only remarkable feature was her eyes. Perhaps she had a squint or a lazy eye. We don't know. The Bible says that her eyes were weak and dull. It is bad enough to have a 'better' older brother or sister. However, I can't help thinking that it must be even harder when the 'perfect' one is younger.

Do you compare yourself with the people around you? Do you feel overshadowed by the success of your brother, a co-worker or a friend? Do you somehow feel that their achievements make you seem awfully small? The enemy always tries to make everyone else's lives look perfect when the reality is usually very different. 2 Corinthians 10:12 says, "For we dare not... compare ourselves..." Remember, there is only one life that you are called to live and it is yours. You are unique and your journey is not a carbon copy of anyone else's. Don't let the devil draw you down the path of making comparisons. It is rarely helpful.

Doubted By Dad

Leah's situation got worse. Her own father Laban doubted that any man would ever want to marry her. So Laban hatched a plan to trick Jacob. Let's stop for a moment and imagine how this young lady must have felt. It was God's plan that sons and daughters should enjoy the affirming affection of their parents. When a child grows up knowing that their father loves them lavishly, it creates security inside. When a little one experiences the attentive delight of their daddy, it affirms their value. That was God's plan for Leah, and it was His plan for you too.

Leah's dad treated his daughter with contempt. Jacob was engaged to be married to Leah's sister, Rachel. The wedding festivities would have included the consumption of much alcohol. Then, late at night, when it was dark, the new bride would be sent to his groom. She would probably have been covered. Laban waited until the end of the day and then sent Leah rather than Rachel into Jacob's tent. Jacob consummated the marriage believing he was with Rachel. When he woke up in the morning, he saw Leah in his bed.

"But in the morning [Jacob saw his wife, and] behold, it was Leah! And he said to Laban, What is this you have done to me? ... Why... have you deceived and cheated and thrown me down [like this]? Genesis 29:25 (AMPC). Leah must have been mortified. Most girls grow up dreaming of a white wedding to Prince Charming. Leah's wedding was not a fairy tale. It must have been more like a nightmare. Jacob made love to Leah believing he was with Rachel. I would not be surprised if the new bride cried herself to sleep that night. She was probably dreading Jacob waking up and discovering the truth.

I know too many sad stories of men and women feeling unwanted in marriage. If that is you, I know it must have been deeply hurtful. We expect that when we meet the 'one', we will enjoy a 'happily ever after'. Sometimes, we can feel forced into marrying the wrong one. That may feel like a life sentence. If you have been rejected by your spouse, God wants to heal your heart.

The young woman already felt second best to her sister. Now she was treated like a piece of meat. In Genesis 29:27 (AMPC), Leah's dad told his son in law to, "Finish the [wedding feast] week [for Leah]; then we will give you [Rachel] also..." Leah must have felt trashed. Her new husband slept with her for a week under compulsion and then won his true love.

Lonely Marriage

Because he was tricked into wedlock, Jacob ended up hating his first wife. Genesis 29:31 (AMPC) says, "...the Lord saw that Leah was despised..." Let me repeat myself. Rejection can make us feel horribly ashamed of ourselves. When someone doesn't want us, it often makes us dislike, and even despise, ourselves. Rejection can all too easily make us feel repulsive.

Leah was married to a man who loved someone else. Jacob adored Leah's little sister. Certain sorts of rejection can hurt more than others. Unrequited love can be devastating, especially when the other person once said, "I do." A loveless marriage is a terribly painful place to live. Perhaps that's your story. Your spouse has grown cold or drifted away. You may see them light up around other people, but they close down with you. Maybe you have become the third member of your marriage as your spouse has strayed. Speaking of infidelity, Proverbs 5:9 tells us not to give our honor to another. If you have suffered the pain of unfaithfulness, you will probably have felt both rejection and shame. Perhaps you keep believing for restoration or maybe you have been replaced by another person.

Broken Promises

The pain of being cast away can be terrible. You could have been jilted at the altar. You believed you were going to enjoy your big day and then the one who promised you everything ended up giving you nothing. Perhaps you did not get that far. You were sure that you had found happiness, but then things fell apart. Your affections grew while theirs faded. The ache on the inside can feel unbearable. Maybe you have never met anyone who wanted to be with you. You may carry the pain of being single in your heart. Not only that, rejection in romantic relationships can make us feel like we must be flawed. It can cause us to doubt our value. It can lead us to wonder, "What's wrong with me? Why am I not enough?" The language that we use illustrates how this kind of rejection can make us feel. When we make statements like, "I was dumped," we are likening ourselves to trash.

Everybody Knows

Public rejection carries added pain. When rejection is common knowledge, there is the added humiliation of everyone knowing your story. Maybe you were openly excluded by friends or family. Perhaps you were unceremoniously fired from your job. You might have been pushed away by your partner or spouse for all to see. Any time anyone looks at you, you may detect pity

43

(or perhaps even scorn) in their eyes. Maybe you are certain that your awful experiences are the topic of other people's conversations. Shame makes us want to crawl away and hide.

Jacob was wealthy so he will have had lots of staff. I'm sure it must have been widely known that Rachel was celebrated while Leah was barely tolerated. The older sister probably endured both scorn and ridicule from family and workers. Even if no-one actually said anything, I'm sure she sensed it inside. She must have felt like a reject. I want to stop for a moment. Remember that Leah is one of the Bible's leading ladies. She birthed half of the Lord's beloved nation and carried the seed of Christ. She was treated like a reject, but she was chosen by God. Does this sound familiar? Speaking of our Savior and King, Psalm 118:22 says, "The stone which the builders rejected has become the chief cornerstone." Leah was despised, but she had an incredible destiny.

God's Decision-Making Process

God chooses the foolish things of this world to confound the wise. As it says in 1 Corinthians 1:28 (AMPC), "God also selected (deliberately chose) what in the world is lowborn and insignificant and branded and treated with contempt, even the things that are nothing..." The rejection that you have suffered may have caused you to question your value. However, God looks for people that others cast aside. He selects those that others snub. He picks those that others count as worthless. He heals their hearts, anoints them with His Spirit and then uses them to bring glory to His name.

Back to Leah. She was desperate to be loved and decided that making her husband a dad would secure his affection. "And Leah became pregnant and bore a son and named him Reuben [See, a son!]; for she said, because the Lord has seen my humiliation and affliction; now my husband will love me" (Genesis 29:32 AMPC). She believed that having children would take away her reproach. Leah convinced herself that once her child arrived, Jacob would love her the way he loved Rachel. But she was looking in the wrong direction for acceptance.

Human Fixes

No human fix can ever change us deep down. A new job cannot wipe away the humiliation of an earlier redundancy. It may build us up temporarily. However, the slightest suggestion of things not going well in our new position may take us straight back to what happened last time. The same is true of romance. If you were rejected by someone you once adored, a new relationship will not make you whole. Of course, being in love again can lift our spirits. But if we see behavior that reminds us of past betrayals, we will probably put the brakes on fast. Time cannot restore. In order for the past to lose its power, we must be healed deep inside.

The arrival of baby Reuben did not change Jacob and it did not heal Leah. Genesis 29:33 in the Amplified tell us, "[Leah] became pregnant again and bore a son and said, because the Lord heard that I am despised, He has given me this son also; and she named him Simeon [God hears]." Our leading lady was still brokenhearted because her husband disliked her. It is hard to give birth at the best of times. If you have gone through labor alone, you may need to be healed. It was God's plan that every mother would have the support of their child's father. If you are a single parent struggling by yourself, the Lord hears the cries of your heart. He is ready to strengthen your soul and lift you up.

Leah then had Levi, still hoping that motherhood would make Jacob fall for her: "Now this time my husband will become attached to me, because I have borne him three sons." (Genesis 29:34b). Leah was desperately trying to win the heart of her husband. When we feel that we are not enough, it can cause us to strive throughout life. The truth is that there is no human affirmation that will ever be sufficient. When we have been ripped apart by rejection, we need to be restored - and deeply assured - by the Lord. We cannot fill our inner vacuums with natural answers. Only God can take away the ache.

Heaven's Answer

Speaking of Jesus, the Message version of Isaiah 53:3 says, "He was looked down on and passed over, a man who suffered, who knew pain firsthand. One look at him and people turned away. We looked down on him, thought he was scum." Jesus understands the pain of scorn. He knows what you have been through and what you are experiencing right now. Not only that, He was publicly punished so that you and I could be restored: "He was beaten so we could be whole. He was whipped so we could be healed." (Isaiah 53:5 NLT). Whipped in the Hebrew is chalal, which means wounded, desecrated, polluted, pierced, or violated. He went through appalling public humiliation so that you could be restored. As we pour out our pain in His presence, He will heal our hearts and fill us up again with His wonderful love.

Something shifted in Leah after she had Levi. She stopped seeking her sufficiency from Jacob. Her eyes moved from man to God. Her marriage was no longer the center of her attention. She looked for a heavenly solution to her longing. We cannot plug our vacuums with human acceptance or affection. Although earthly love and companionship can help for a while, they do not offer lasting relief. When we have not dealt with the roots of rejection, no amount of love will be enough. Please ask the Lord to heal every remnant of rejection so that you can be stable and secure.

The Truth Of The Matter

When the truth of Colossians 2:10 sank deep into my heart, it changed my life. It says, "...you are complete in Him..." Let me explain... With Jesus, you are enough. You are sufficient in Him. You are already adequate in Christ. I encourage you to quit striving and instead accept that you are complete in Him. You do not need a human solution to make you acceptable because you are already enough. In reality, while we are still carrying the wounds of rejection, it can be hard to believe this verse. If you were treated in ways that suggested you were insignificant, it will be important to allow the Lord to heal your heart first. At the end of this chapter, I will lead you in prayer. Once the pain is taken away, the lies that we have believed become easy to dismiss. Then you will be able to allow the truth to change you like it changed me.

The New Leah

Genesis 29:35 (NIV) highlights the change in Leah: "She conceived again, and when she gave birth to a son she said, 'This time I will praise the Lord.' So she named him Judah." Leah was God's chosen vessel to birth and raise Judah. 1 Corinthians 1:28 (AMPC) reveals the heart of God for those of us who others spurn: "And God also selected (deliberately chose) what in the world is lowborn and insignificant and branded and treated with contempt, even the things that are nothing, that He might depose and bring to nothing the things that are." God picked Leah for a powerful purpose. However, He waited until she was ready to fulfill her destiny.

Let us deal with the pain and shame of every rejection that is still weighing us down. Tell the Lord how being shunned made you feel. As you talk about the impact it had on your heart and your life, you will dislodge buried pain. As the hurt surfaces and you "... pour out your heart like water before the face of

47

the Lord..." (Lamentations 2:19b), God will reach deep down and bring wonderful healing. The shame will melt away. Let's pray.

Heavenly Father,

I have been pushed away by people I admire, and it hurts. (Now tell the Lord exactly what happened in as much detail as possible. Explain who rejected you and how it made you feel. Tell Him how much it hurt.) Being unwanted was bad enough, but it also made me feel like a complete fool. The whole experience was humiliating. (Share every sense of shame in prayer. If you were publicly pushed away, explain how it affected your view of yourself. Talk to the Lord as you would a close confidant.) I bring all my rejection and every ounce of shame to you. What I have hidden for fear of greater humiliation, I now bring into the light of Your love. As I pour out all my pain, heal my heart, oh Lord.

Thank You that I am enough for You. Thank You that I do not need to strive for Your love and acceptance. Thank You that in Your eyes, I am already sufficient. I will no longer strive for human affirmation or for human fixes. Your love and Your acceptance is enough for me. (Now linger in the presence of God and allow the Lord to fill you afresh with His wonderful love).

I love You with all my heart and I give you all the glory, Lord, for what You are doing in my life.

In Jesus' name, I pray,

Amen.

Chapter 5

ROOTS

My husband Paul grew up in one of the worst neighborhoods in Britain. Most of the young men on his street ended up on drugs, in prison, or dead. The area was so rough that his zip code was notorious with the local police force. His family was among the poorest of the poor. My husband's sister slept in a drawer because they could not afford a cot while he wore second-hand clothes until he was a teenager. The family didn't have the money for hot water so Paul only had a bath every three months. At school, he was disliked because he smelled.

The ugliness of poverty imprinted itself on Paul's identity. His address put an invisible boundary around any ambitions. Constant hardship and lack made Paul think that his life had no value. After he was saved, God had to heal my husband in the depths of his identity. It wasn't just the way that he was treated that hurt him. Poverty itself made him believe he was worthless.

The Stigma Of Lack

Ezekiel 36:30 (AMPC) mentions "...the reproach and disgrace of famine..." Poverty is foul. It makes people feel ashamed of themselves. Reproach means discredit or disapproval. Prosperity can seem like a stamp of approval on a person's life. The impressive car, the imposing home and the important job all tell a story of success. In contrast, poverty can feel like a public disgrace. It is hard to hide lack. It may seem as though the whole world knows. Somehow that can make it even more degrading.

People can be cruel. If your views have been dismissed because of your lack or if you have been put down because of poverty, it may have heightened a sense of worthlessness. You need to know that God's desire is for your restoration. Psalms 113:7 (AMPC) says, "[The Lord] raises the poor out of the dust and lifts the needy from the ash heap..." He wants the best for you. He will make a way where there seems to be no way. And it is not only that. God takes it personally when you are mistreated: "He who mocks the poor reproaches his Maker..." (Proverbs 17:5). The Lord feels insulted when someone belittles you. We are all His handiwork, of immense (but equal) value: "The rich and the poor have this in common, The Lord is the maker of them all." (Proverbs 22:2)

If the stigma of lack is upon us, it can be hard to rise out of poverty into true prosperity. Shame tries to convince us that we deserve to be broke. It pigeonholes us as poor. Proverbs 23:7 explains the problem with this mindset: "For as he thinks in his heart, so is he..." If you judge yourself as unworthy of God's blessings, you may keep yourself in a position of need. If you think that hardship is your lot in life, your beliefs will keep you bound. Until our inner convictions change, it will be almost impossible to break out of poverty.

Your Upbringing

It is not just lack that can constrain us. Sometimes our upbringing makes us feel small. God told Prophet Samuel that Saul would be Israel's first king in 1 Samuel 9:17: "There he is, the man of whom I spoke to you. This one shall reign over My people."

When Samuel shared the exciting news with Saul, he was stunned. "And Saul answered and said, 'Am I not a Benjamite, of the smallest of the tribes of Israel, and my family the least of all the families of the tribe of Benjamin? Why then do you speak like this to me?'" (1 Samuel 9:21). You can hear the disbelief in Saul's response. He believed his upbringing disqualified him. He saw himself as a nobody which made him reject the suggestion that he could lead. In his opinion, his roots made him insignificant. He believed he was not of the right pedigree for prominence.

Hiding The Signs

Do you try to hide your accent? Maybe you avoid mentioning the name of your neighborhood to new people. Do you ever feel like your nation makes you less valuable than someone from another country? Are you embarrassed about your upbringing? Jesus knows how it feels. John 1:45-46 reads: "Philip found Nathanael and said to him, 'We have found Him of whom Moses in the law, and also the prophets, wrote-Jesus of Nazareth, the son of Joseph.' And Nathanael said to him, "Can anything good come out of Nazareth?"'

Nazareth was an obscure little hill town. It was remote and insignificant. As a result, Nathanael struggled to believe that Jesus could be the Messiah. How could someone of value come from somewhere so inconsequential? The world all too often tries to suggest that your address determines your destiny. They did it to the Son of God and maybe they have done it you. It is wrong, it is cruel, and it is hurtful. Let me make something clear. No race or ethnicity, no color or class, no accent or social standing impresses God. Man looks at the outward appearance, but God looks at your heart (1 Samuel 16:7b). It is not your nation and it is not your neighborhood that decides your station in life. Proverbs 4:23 (NLT) makes the truth clear, "Guard your heart above all else, for it determines the course of your life." The story of King Solomon's wife is told in the Song of Songs. She suffered from insecurity as a result of her upbringing. If you have been wounded on your journey through life, I encourage you to get hold of my book 'Lifting the Mask', which describes how this woman is eventually healed.

The Pain of Prejudice

Sometimes the rejection runs deep. If you have repeatedly experienced prejudice, it could have eroded your view of your value. Put-downs, hurtful assumptions and callous comments can crush our confidence. Maybe you were made to feel inferior because your family was uneducated. Perhaps you were mocked because you wore second-hand or cheap clothes while peers were dressed in designer outfits. If anything about your background makes you feel like a second-class citizen, it will be important to allow the Lord to heal your heart. Once the pain has gone, we can ask God to break every lie you have believed.

I encourage you to confront every attempt of the enemy to use your upbringing to make you feel unqualified. It is a lie. Once you are healed, the only power it has is the power we give it by listening to it. 3 John 1:2 says, "Beloved, I pray that you may prosper in all things and be in health, just as your soul prospers." Notice that God's desire is that we prosper to the extent that our souls prosper. The more we allow the Lord to do inside us, the more we will see the blessings of God in other arenas of our lives.

Let's go back to the story of Saul. The Lord considered all the eligible people in Israel and He chose Saul to be the nation's first king. That's the best endorsement anyone could ever ask for. The God of heaven and earth selected Saul. However, Saul's feelings of inferiority made him want to run from his calling. Even on the day of his coronation, when the time came for him to be presented to the people he was hiding. 1 Samuel 10:21-23 says, '...But when they sought him, he could not be found. Therefore they inquired of the Lord further, "Has the man come here yet?" And the Lord answered, "There he is, hidden among the equipment."' What a ridiculous situation: the soon-to-be-coronated king of Israel was hiding behind the equipment. Saul was trying to avoid his calling because he felt unqualified. Shame always makes us want to hide. It tries to stop us from stepping forward. We need to uproot any sense of inadequacy so that we can freely fulfill our destiny.

The World's Value System

It is sad to see how the media covers major tragedies around the world. I once saw a tiny story on page 18 of a leading London newspaper about a boat that sank off the coast of Gabon, killing 200 people. If that ship had capsized off the coast of California, it would almost certainly have been front page news. However, 'first world' lives were not lost. Men, women and children from an impoverished, war-torn nation in Africa died. Their lives were treated by the media as though they were less valuable. When we are bombarded by messages telling us that our upbringing somehow reduces our value, we can all too easily end up believing that such fake news is true.

Sticky Circumstances

Myra was raised in a volatile home. Her parents were always arguing. Myra's father was not faithful and the infidelity was destroying her mother. Night after night, the couple would hurl insults at each other while Myra listened from the top of the stairs. Eventually, Myra's mother left her father. Several years later, Myra's dad married another woman who had a child the same age as Myra. The two went to high school together. Myra's friends all seemed to come from perfect families. This made her feel second-rate. She was embarrassed about her parents' divorce and felt that her family history made her flawed.

Myra was so ashamed of her background that she invented a different story. She told her friends that her stepsister was in fact her sister and led even her closest companions to believe that her stepmother was her real mum. Even when they asked how she could have a sister who was so close to her in age, she dismissed their questions. Myra believed that her fractured family made her inferior. She was so ashamed of her life that she made up lies to cover the truth. As I ministered, God began a deep work of healing in this precious lady's heart. The Lord healed deep inner wounds as Myra acknowledged for the first time that she had been abandoned by her mother. This led to a life-changing healing journey. Through our Healed for Life conferences, God took away every sense of shame and set Myra's life on a bright new course. She is now free and can be honest about her circumstances in all situations.

Facing The Truth

It is time to face every issue from your background. If you have carried any shame because of your roots, it will be important to allow the Lord to heal your heart. If you have felt less valuable because of poverty, it is time to be restored. If you feel that your family, your city, or your nation somehow makes you inferior, it is time to demolish the devil's lies. I would love to lead you in prayer.

Heavenly Father,

I realize that my upbringing has made me feel ashamed. I thought my background made me inferior (Now tell the Lord about your family, your upbringing, or your nation. Explain - in as much detail as possible - exactly what it is about your story that has marked you. Tell the Lord how you feel about your background). Lord, please heal my heart of every shred of shame. Take away the pain of every mocking word and sense of insignificance.

Now, Lord, I choose to believe Your word. I destroy every lie that I have believed. Thank You that I am made in Your image and You are great. Thank You that I am Your handiwork and that You have a wonderful plan for my life to prosper me and not to harm me, to give me a hope and a bright future. Thank You that I am precious in Your sight.

I give You all the glory.

In Jesus' name,

Amen.

Chapter 6

ABUSE

At the tender age of twelve, Terry's world was torn apart. He woke up in the dead of the night at boarding school to find an older student on top of him. Terrified, Terry was about to cry out when the man muffled his mouth and threatened him: "If you breathe a word to anyone, I will kill you." He froze until the terrible ordeal ended and the man left. Terry lay awake traumatized for most of the night, unable to fathom what had just happened. "I felt dirty and lost," Terry explained. "My thoughts were confused. I could not comprehend what had just happened."

After some disturbed sleep, Terry got up early in the morning. He hurried to the bathroom to wash himself, desperate to remove the filthy feeling. He then headed for home, certain that his father would know how to help. But his dad did not ask why his little boy looked so broken. Instead, he scolded his son for being out of lessons and sent him back to school. A couple of weeks later, Terry was raped by another man. In total, he was raped five times before he was fourteen.

Proverbs 10:23 says, "To do evil is like sport to a fool..." Like Terry, maybe you've experienced cruel games being played by the people around you. If you felt like the prey while others appeared to be predators, God wants to heal every hurt in your heart. I don't know what you have gone through, but I do know that your Heavenly Father is able to restore. Perhaps you were abused by people who should have protected you. Maybe you were raped (even repeatedly). You could have been molested or assaulted. You may have been the victim of violence or even torture. Whatever you have gone through, I want you to know that you can come out the other side fully restored. This chapter is for you. Let's go back to Terry's story.

The End Of The World As I Knew It

Life - as Terry knew it - was over. Days merged into weeks and weeks into months, but the pain remained. "I was numb and felt totally alone," Terry shared. "I had frequent flashbacks and I couldn't sleep at night for fear of being attacked again. The repeated rapes made me feel like a piece of meat. I was there to be taken by anyone. I surrendered myself to fate. The only protection I had was to give in. I could not speak to anyone about it. I hated every single moment."

Terry attempted suicide twice. When he was twelve, he took tablets and collapsed. Thankfully, he was rushed to hospital. At fourteen, he tried to suffocate himself. The Lord alone preserved his life. Terry was then expelled from school for doing badly in his exams. More rejection bound up with another layer of shame crushed this traumatized teenager even further. He became extremely angry. Rage boiled inside. He started to fight with his dad. He was completely out of control and felt no connection with anyone.

When Terry was sixteen, he met Vivian, the woman who would become his wife. She came from a broken family and was extremely timid. "I first hit Vivian when we were both eighteen and it carried on into our marriage. I was volatile. I could not take no for an answer and would explode anytime she disagreed with me. Every time I hit or pushed Vivian, she would break down and cry. She somehow accepted me - and all of my cruelty - but I hated myself." On one occasion, Terry's neighbors called the police, but Vivian would not press charges.

A New Start But Not A New Heart

Terry gave his life to the Lord in 1994 and never hit his wife again. Although God's love was chipping away at his heart, he was still filled with shame and rage. The words that came out of Terry's mouth were his new weapons. He became verbally abusive. Vivian's self-worth was already in shreds from years of childhood rejection, so his cruel comments just confirmed her view of herself. "You're stupid," Terry would yell with scorn. "Look at you. You're nothing!" Terry dominated his wife and their three children were terrified of him.

The Turnaround

When he was in his early thirties, Terry attended his first healing conference. Sitting in a small group, my husband Paul had a word of knowledge that someone was carrying the burden of a painful childhood memory. For the first time in the twenty years since the brutal assaults, Terry shared his story. He broke down and wept. That marked the start of his healing journey. Ecclesiastes 3:1-4 tells us that God has set apart a time for healing: "To everything there is a season, a time for every purpose under heaven... a time to break down... a time to weep..." We prepare for our restoration by facing the truth that we have tried so hard to avoid. More often than not, healing itself begins when we open up and tears flow. Suppressed pain comes pouring out. If you feel buried sadness surfacing, please don't push it back down. Pain is always better out than in.

"It was as though a heavy backpack was lifted off my shoulders," Terry explained. "The atmosphere was thick with love and genuine acceptance. I was surrounded by Christian brothers and sisters. Then my spiritual father gave me a hug. I had been heard for the first time. The shame was shifting as my pain was brought into the light."

On another occasion, Terry and Vivian sat with my husband and I in our home. We talked about their marriage and his past. Terry broke down and wept from the depths of his soul. This was his second supernatural healing encounter. The shame that had cloaked Terry for more than twenty years lifted.

God continued working on Terry over the next decade until all the hidden hurts were healed and every trace of shame was removed. The Lord also restored Vivian. This once broken couple now run Harvest Church London's marriage ministry, which brings restoration to relationships and families. Terry is head of prayer for Healed for Life and a leader who is being used to bring God's healing love to the nations.

Kicking Back

Shame causes us to react. Sometimes we retreat and hide. Often we are extremely angry. At times we shut down inside. Occasionally, like Terry did for a season, we kick back. In Psalm 119:143 (NLT), the writer describes the build-up: "...pressure and stress bear down on me..." When we are squashed by abuse or violence, it can create an almost irresistible urge to lash out. God made us in His image. His plan is that His precious sons and daughters are treated with care and dignity. When we are degraded or defiled, something inside can snap.

I was never part of the in-crowd at school. I usually had a few friends, but I was generally more tolerated than celebrated. In kindergarten, I was disliked by many and despised by some. Girls in my class treated me like a reject. I felt ugly and unwanted. For weeks, I endured terrible feelings of shame. Then one day, when two girls were teasing me, I snapped. At just six years of age, I grabbed them both by their hair and smashed their heads together! They screamed, cried and then called the teachers.

In truth, I think I was as shocked as they were. I had no idea that I could behave that way. I was just a little girl who couldn't handle shame. Unfortunately, hitting back never helps. Instead, guilt usually builds. As a result, we often end up with even greater levels of shame. Perhaps when you look over your life, you realize that kicking back became your habit. Maybe you became violent or displayed regular outbursts of rage. The way we react can make us feel like we don't deserve to be healed of our hurts. That is a lie. There is nothing that you have done that has placed you outside of the boundaries of God's love. You are His child. He cares deeply about you. He wants to heal your heart and keep it healed.

Too Broke To Fix

One of the enemy's terrible lies is to convince God's people that there are some things that are so bad that we can never fully recover from them. Satan tries to make us believe that we have to limp our way silently through life. You may assume that the best you can expect is to forgive and try to forget. Perhaps you have accepted that you will always feel some sadness beneath the surface. Let me give you an example to explain. If you were repeatedly raped, you may believe you can forgive and move on. However, you might doubt that you can ever truly enjoy marital intimacy.

I have heard many people say that you can never fully recover from the loss of a child. After all, you are supposed to lay your parents to rest at some point, but you should never bury your babies. I want you to know that this is untrue. I am not saying that healing is instant or always easy, but Jesus paid the price for our total restoration from every painful situation.

Our first child Naomi died very suddenly, just before her second birthday. My husband and I were devastated. About four weeks after the dreadful day, her doctor visited us at our home. There had been medical negligence in the last twenty four hours of her life, so he wanted to be sure that we understood what had gone wrong. Hospital procedures were eventually changed to try to ensure that no other child would die in similar circumstances. While the consultant was with us, he made a strong statement. He told us that we would never get over the death of our daughter. His intention was to demonstrate that he understood the depths of our agony. But in truth, he was horribly wrong.

Whose Report Will You Believe?

When human understanding (however compassionate it may sound) contradicts God's word, we must make a choice. Isaiah 53:1 asks us whose report we will believe. There are numerous verses about the healing power of God. Psalm 147:3 (AMPC) says, "He heals the brokenhearted and binds up their wounds [curing their pains and their sorrows]." The Hebrew for heal in this verse is raphah and it means to mend, to cure, to make whole; šâbar is the Hebrew for broken and it means crushed, destroyed, broken in pieces.

The picture being painted here is of irreparable damage. God promises you and I that He can - and will - heal our most horrendous hurts. My life was shattered after the death of my daughter. God did what man could not do. Over the weeks and months after our little girl went to be with the Lord, He reached into the depths of my being and pulled my pain out. He healed me and He healed my husband.

Terry's soul was smashed into a thousand pieces. He was beyond human help. Our loving Heavenly Father healed this precious man's heart, piece by piece. God poured His liquid love into every part of Terry's heart until he was made whole. What the Lord did for Terry and his wife He will do for you.

Why Is It So Very Painful?

Abuse is the wrongful or improper treatment of a person. It is treating someone in a way that they were never designed to be treated. It is degrading and demeaning. It strips its victims of their dignity. When someone overrides the will of another human being, it makes that person feel as if part of their humanity has been stolen. Perhaps your life was good until one terrible trauma left you crushed. You may have felt that your innocence was taken. Maybe abuse was not a one time experience. Your life might have been a catalogue of neglect and assaults. I want you to know that God is able to heal your heart.

Shame produces a host of toxic and debilitating emotions. People deal with these in many different ways. You are unique and so are your reactions to mistreatment. Having said that, there are certain telltale patterns. Perhaps you boil with rage. Maybe you become terribly anxious and confused. You might be overwhelmed with humiliation or disgust. You may feel disgraced. Perhaps you blame yourself and feel terrible guilt. You could have shut down to the world around you. It might be that you cower when you are around certain types of people. You may crave love and go from one bad relationship to another. Do you become aggressive, releasing anger towards those you love the most? Or you might have trouble trusting people.

Trust Issues

Many years ago, I had the privilege of knowing a wonderful worship leader who had traveled on a hard journey through life. Her childhood was marred by terrible neglect. After being saved and nurtured into church leadership, she was badly hurt by a poisonous split in the congregation. This woman then experienced betrayal in marriage. When she shared her painful experiences with me, the words that saddened me the most were: "I trust no one." The enemy used her experiences to try to limit her opportunities for future happiness.

You may think that mistrust is an inevitable and harmless part of life. You could even believe that it is helpful. Of course, we need to discern who is trustworthy. It is also true that trust is earned. However, being unable to trust is a lonely place to live. Let me explain. The Creator of the universe knows our flaws and failings, and yet He trusts us. We were made in His image, which means we were designed to trust. When we are wounded by those who should have protected us, it can erode our faith in people. The enemy seeks to keep us trapped in a world of pain. God wants to heal your heart deep down so that slowly - but surely - you can start to trust again.

Thawed Heart

Sofia was abused by her father from as young as she can remember. It only stopped when he was sent to prison. Both Sofia's mom and her aunt knew what he was doing but chose to turn a blind eye. They did not protect this precious little girl from unbearable abuse.

Perhaps that is your story: people knew what you were going through and did not help. That pain can be almost as awful as the abuse itself. Proverbs 16:30 (AMPC) says, "He who shuts his eyes to... perverse things and who compresses his lips [as if in concealment] brings evil to pass." If that was your story, God wants to heal both the pain of every attack as well as the agony of knowing certain people ignored what was happening. Let us return to Sofia's story.

While her dad was in prison, Sofia's mom - who was now mentally ill - became violent and controlling. Although her extended family realized what she was going through, they did nothing. It was as though the world refused to help. As an adult, the flashbacks haunted Sofia and she turned to drink and drugs in an attempt to numb the pain. She then went from meaningless relationship to meaningless relationship, trying to fill the hole in her heart. This led to a web of shame, guilt and self-rejection. People who were meant to protect her had brought nothing but devastation. Sofia hardened her heart, wore a mask and kept everyone at a distance. Until her healing journey began.

Pulling Out The Pain

Sofia explained: "At Healed for Life, God pulled pain out of the depths of my heart and filled my empty places with His love. I cried and sobbed. It felt like I was pouring out the pain in my heart in every tear. My hardness melted and I kept being filled afresh with God's healing love. Back home, I began to change and soften. Memories came, but they did not haunt me like before. The Lord showed me that He was with me from the start. He revealed how He rescued me even when my own family turned a blind eye. He was with me through it all and He is with me now. He is always with me.

"I am still on a journey," Sofia continued, "but emotional shackles fall away with every step I take. I can run faster and bolder and

I am now living the life of freedom He intended for me. Healed for Life is not a one-time hit. It is a journey. So I keep going. I am no longer ruled by my past but pressing towards my future. God's hand is on my life and I am overwhelmed by how He has blessed me in so many ways."

King David's Daughter

Tamar was King David's daughter. She was a princess with a bright future. All too often, terrible things happen to good individuals. I think that is because the devil detests nice people. Well, something horrible happened to this young lady. Her awful story is told in 2 Samuel 13. Tamar's half-brother Amnon had an obsessive crush on her. He was so consumed with having his wicked way with her that he made himself sick with unfulfilled lust.

God created sex to be a loving and pleasurable bond between a husband and wife. It was intended to be a fruitful blessing. The enemy is always seeking to spoil sex. He tries to get people into bed outside of wedlock and then attempts to keep them out of bed once they are married. A healthy physical bond can be a powerful unifier so satan is always seeking to steal and smear our sexuality. Just as God wants to heal our hearts, He also wants to restore our purity. When He restores, He makes us brand new. If you have been hurt in this area of your life, God wants to deal with the shame and the pain.

Amnon tricked Tamar into his bedroom. This precious young woman could not have anticipated what was about to happen. Amnon was her brother so she probably trusted him. Sadly, he was hell-bent on hurting her. Amnon sent everyone away so that he could be alone with his sister. Then he forced her to have sex with him. Tamar pleaded with her brother to stop. No amount of anguish would deter him. Amnon raped Tamar. In one horrific attack, Tamar's life changed forever. She was brutally betrayed by the brother she was trying to help. She was robbed of her innocence.

Naming Shame

There is something so unbearable about shame that at times we don't even want to name the things that made us feel so defiled. After Amnon raped Tamar, he told her to get out of his sight. Tamar pleaded with her brother: "'No, indeed! This evil of sending me away is worse than the other that you did to me.' But he would not listen to her." (2 Samuel 13:16). Tamar could not bring herself to name rape. Instead, she said, "... the other that you did..." Admitting what had happened was too awful. In her heart, shame made the rape unspeakable.

Shame makes us want to hide from what happened. Perhaps you went through something that you have struggled to speak about. Maybe you feel as though talking will bring you back to the event. Shame smears us. It makes us feel dirty. We want to run away from the memory that caused us to feel defiled. As a result, we often avoid talking about the events that led to our distress. We try to distance ourselves from the experiences and the way they made us feel.

There is a problem with this. As long as our darkest memories remain hidden in the closets of our hearts, they have the power to cause pain. When we make the brave decision to bring them into the light, we loosen their grip on our lives. Ephesians 5:13 in the Passion Translation says, "Whatever the revelation-light exposes, it will also correct..." When we bring our pain into the light, we begin the process of evicting shame from our hearts.

At a women's conference several years ago, the Lord gave me an unexpected instruction. He asked me to invite people to stand who had been abused, molested or raped. I struggled at first. Then God showed me why. The enemy keeps victims of sexual mistreatment bound by shame. Suddenly anger arose on the inside. How dare the devil make a victim feel ashamed? The pain alone is bad enough for anyone to bear. It is not that I want perpetrators to be ashamed; I long for them to be saved and sanctified. However, it is abhorrent to think that someone who has been abused should feel the need to hide what happened. They need to be helped, not hidden away. I was amazed at what happened in that auditorium. About one third of the entire conference stood and then came to the altar. Women wept as they embraced one another. There was a supernatural move of healing and shame was driven away.

The Dark Cloak

Shame is like a dark cloak. It attaches itself to us and then we don't know how to make it go away. When she pleaded with her brother not to defile her, Tamar asked, "As for me, where could I take my shame?" This phrase says so much. Shame is like a dirty rag that fixes itself to us. We want to push it away, but we don't know how. The Amplified version expresses the verse above like this: "How could I rid myself of my shame?" Everything the enemy does is either a counterfeit or the demonic opposite of one of God's gifts. Shame is the opposite of honor. Understanding honor will help us to grasp the foul nature of shame and how to be free from its smear.

Psalm 8:4-5 says, "What is man that You are mindful of him... You have crowned him with glory and honor." The Hebrew word translated here as honor is 'hadar'. The noun comes from a verb that means to make splendid or adorn with glory. It is something that someone does to dignify another person. The Creator of heaven and earth covers us with glory and honor. When you gave your life to the Lord, He cloaked you with His goodness. He placed a crown on your head and adorned you with beauty.

The Lord knows our vulnerability, so He covers us with His dignity. He understands the weakness of our humanity, so He clothes us with His glory. God does not want to expose our inadequacies. Rather, He seeks to protect us. Shame is the demonic counterfeit of honor. One makes us cower, while the other makes us courageous. Shame covers us with dishonor. It clothes us with disgrace. While shrouded all around, we are left feeling exposed. When we realize that shame is the enemy's cloak, it can help us develop the determination to strip it from our lives.

Soiled

Amnon's reaction to Tamar after the assault made the terrible pain even worse. He had defiled himself, as well as his sister, and he was disgusted. As a result, he could not stand being near her. Amnon commanded his servant, "Put this woman out, away from me, and bolt the door behind her." (2 Samuel 13:17). Shame smeared both the perpetrator and victim. Amnon had his servant throw his sister the princess out of his house. She was traumatized and must have been very frightened. Like a soiled cloth, shame makes us feel dirty. It feels like an indelible stain that we can't clean away. Amnon's actions must have made her feel even more repulsed - not only at him, but also at herself.

I Don't Like Myself

One of the worst effects of shame is that all too often it causes self-hatred. It fixes itself to us and makes us feel unclean. As a result, we blame ourselves. We reject ourselves. We hate ourselves. Perhaps those words are too strong to describe your inner view. However, any amount of self-loathing is destructive. It makes us think we don't deserve to be healed. It makes us believe we are not worthy of love. If you don't like yourself, you may push away the very people who can help. In order to be free, you need to reach a place of self-acceptance.

Perhaps you see yourself as different. I don't mean that you believe you are wonderfully unique. I mean that you think others are better than you. You might see yourself as an outsider or even an outcast. You could view yourself as a fraud or even a freak. When we dislike ourselves, we often hear an inner narrative that tells us we can't succeed. Perhaps your thoughts haunt you with statements such as: "Who do you think you are?" or "You'll never make it." Even when things are going well, you might put yourself down: "This won't work out the way I want. You are going to mess this up like you always do..." In our most important relationships, that voice shouts from within, "He doesn't really love you." Or, "Why would she want to be your friend? There must be something wrong with her." Hatred is harmful. It is an offspring of satan and it punishes its victims.

When we dislike ourselves, we often refuse help. Proverbs 15:32 in the Amplified says, "He who refuses and ignores instruction... despises himself..." We may sabotage positive relationships and push away support. Ecclesiastes 2:17 in the Message says: "I hate life. As far as I can see, what happens on earth is... bad..." God understands the traumas that may have caused you to despise yourself. He is able to bring you into freedom.

True Love

The New Testament tells us eight times to love our neighbors just as we love ourselves (Matthew 19:19, Matthew 22:39, Mark 12:31, Mark 12:33, Luke 10:27, Romans 13:9, Galatians 5:14, James 2:8). Our ability to really love others flows from our God-given love and acceptance of ourselves. God is love. We are made in His image. His intention was (and still is) for us to be loved, to receive love and to show love. If you reject yourself, God wants to pull out that pain and heal your heart.

If you realize that you dislike (or even hate) yourself, how will you ever be able to love your neighbor properly? I encourage you to acknowledge that right now. We will deal with the pain of defilement, but first we need to confront every ounce of self-hatred. My husband helps me in many ways. One example is that he always describes things exactly as they are. If I am being lazy or selfish, he will call it out. That helps me to get wrong attitudes out of my life. It is always better to name and shame sin. That way we can walk away free. We are commanded to love, not hate. That makes self-loathing a sin. I want to encourage you to recognize that self-hatred is wrong. If you don't like yourself, please join me in a prayer of repentance:

Heavenly Father,

Thank you that You love me and You have a good plan for my life. I realize that traumatic experiences have led me to dislike myself. I have viewed myself as inadequate and unpleasant. (If you realize that your view of yourself has been very harsh, continue with the next sentence:) I have even despised myself and loathed my life. Today I repent of all self-hatred. I ask You to forgive me for despising myself and for rejecting myself. You love me and You accept me, so I choose today to love myself and I choose to accept myself. Holy Spirit, I ask for Your help. Please enable me to see myself the way my Father in heaven sees me. Thank You that I was made to be loved by You and the people around me, so I also choose to love myself.

In Jesus' name, I pray,

Amen.

As God heals the traumas that cause you to dislike yourself, it will become easier to allow love to flow. If you struggled with the prayer we just prayed, please stay on your healing journey. We have seen countless people break free from self-hatred at our conferences as their hearts were healed.

Your Release Valve

Let's get back to Tamar. After Amnon threw his sister out of the house, she felt ashamed, rejected and heartbroken. She ran from Amnon's home in floods of tears. She turned to another brother, Absalom.

God gave us a powerful release mechanism called crying. When we weep, we offload sorrow and sadness. King David, one of the Bible's greatest heroes and strongest leaders, cried regularly: "... All night I make my bed swim; I drench my couch with my tears." (Psalms 6:6). Joseph wept many times: so loudly that the neighbors heard and for so long that he stained his cheeks red. Joseph cried in the arms of his father and as he embraced his brothers. Jeremiah spoke of his tears before the Lord and encouraged the people of Israel to cry. Jesus wept and Paul sobbed. These healthy biblical role models knew how to release sadness and give their pain to God. Crying is normal and healthy.

Tamar was doing the only thing that she could do at that time. She was weeping. There is no doubt that it was the right thing to do. If she had only continued - following in her father David's footsteps and telling the Lord about every agony and the pain within - I believe God would have healed her heart. Absalom did not know how to help his sister. He loved her, but he did not know how to take her pain away. Instead of sitting down with Tamar, listening to her anguish and speaking kindly to her, Absalom said: "But now hold your peace, my sister. He is your brother; do not take this thing to heart." This was horribly wrong for three reasons.

What Peace?

First, Absalom told Tamar to hold her peace. Tamar was broken in pieces. There was no peace to hold. How many times have you heard people say this in awful situations? Second, Absalom suggested his sister should ignore the issue because the perpetrator was her brother. Many people have a deep sense of loyalty that makes them think that they must protect family privacy at all costs. If you have been hurt by your nearest and dearest, the Lord wants to heal you. It is not dishonoring to admit to God that you were wounded by your relatives. In fact, it is essential that you are honest with God and ask Him to heal you.

Absalom's third statement was ridiculous. Tamar was a mess. This brutal attack had torn her apart. Yet her brother advised her not to take this matter to heart. He was implying that she should stop crying and push down her pain. He told her to internalize her hurt. Perhaps he could not handle the agony of seeing his sister like this. Maybe he thought that showing sadness was a sign of weakness. It could be that he believed tears would give Amnon another victory. The very next phrase is so sad. " So, Tamar remained desolate." (2 Samuel 13:20b).

Shut Down

Tamar shut down on the inside. She shut the world out and she shut her mouth. Then she remained desolate for the rest of her life. Tamar never dealt with her pain. As a direct result, the Bible suggests that her destiny was derailed. Sweeping sadness under the carpet does not make it go away. Turning our eyes away from trauma will not make the shame go away. Society often tells us to hide our emotions. Culture teaches us that silence is strength and that emotional detachment from our distress is a sign of maturity. It can be difficult to pour out our pain to God, but the rewards are relief and freedom. The fruit is lasting fulfillment.

God has a great plan for your life - to prosper you and give you a bright future. It is important that you know this. However, the devil has a plan too. According to John 10:10, satan wants to kill, steal and destroy. He knows he can't just waltz in and end all our lives. So he tries to spoil them. Satan seeks to destroy your destiny. He knows that your heart determines the course of your life, so he will do everything in his power to keep you constrained by pain and shame.

Shutting Out Help

When we have been wounded, we often close our hearts. Our protective shutters come down and we build invisible barriers. Psalms 17:10 says: "They have closed up their... hearts." Please realize that although these walls may make you feel safe for a season, in the long run they also keep you from the healing love of God. He wants you to open up in His presence so that He can heal you of every hurt. The devil wants you to live in a prison of sadness and fear. The enemy is always whispering lies to make you shut down. However, when we open our hearts to the Lord, it is amazing the freedom we can find.

Trapped Words

The Bible tells us to share our innermost issues with the Lord in prayer: "Pour out your heart like water before the face of the Lord." Lamentations 2:19b. When we pour out our heart to a friend, we tell them what has been weighing us down. We share our secrets. That is what we need to do with God. When we tell Him what happened to us and how much it hurt, it helps unlock buried pain. As we speak the words we never said (because we felt we couldn't), we release healing tears in the presence of God. When we tell God how stained or ashamed we really feel, we give Him access to our hearts. The Lord instructs us to deal with all sadness: "...Remove sorrow from your heart." (Ecclesiastes 11:10). The only way I know how to remove sorrow is by pouring out my sadness before God in prayer. He can then reach into the depths of our souls, take away our shame and release His healing love.

They Knew...

Tamar's father heard about what happened, but it would appear that he did nothing. This must have been like another stab in the back for this young girl. Assault is agonizing enough. However, when the people you would have expected to help do nothing, it can make the wound even worse. We talked about this earlier in the chapter, but it is a very real hurt that needs healing. Proverbs 16:30 (AMPC) says, "He who shuts his eyes to... perverse things and who compresses his lips [as if in concealment] brings evil to pass." If you have been hurt by family members turning a blind eye or by friends failing to help, God wants to heal your heart.

When people all around you have let you down, it can be difficult to trust even God. We wonder where He was when everything was going wrong. In truth, He is the only one who can help, so it is important to open our hearts to Him. The most common Hebrew word for trust is bâṭaḥ. In essence, it means to put your confidence in something or someone. Psalm 4:5b says, "Put your trust in the Lord." Please know that although people have failed you, God will not let you down. Psalms 9:10 explains: "Those who know Your name will put their trust in You..." A person's name represents their reputation or integrity. This scripture is saying that those who really know God know they can trust Him. You can trust the Lord to heal your heart.

Walls All Around

Proverbs 18:1 says, "A man who isolates himself seeks his own desire; he rages against all wise judgment." The enemy wants you to isolate yourself. He wants to cut you off from destiny relationships and cause you to close down. When you keep people at arm's length, you deny yourself the joy of relationships. You also lock away the gift that you are and the gifts that are family, friends and the church. As you begin to heal, those isolating walls will come tumbling down.

Violence

Joseph is one of the Old Testament's best known and best loved heroes. But he had a tough life. At just seventeen years of age, he was beaten by his brothers and kicked into a pit. He cried for their help from the bottom of the pit but they ignored his desperate pleas. Instead they sat down and ate a meal (see Genesis 37:23-25). Joseph must have been devastated.

When we are physically abused, our bodies may be in great pain. However, I think the blows to our souls probably run deeper. Whenever our will is overridden, it makes us feel stripped of our dignity. Being assaulted all too often makes you feel like a fool. The attackers are all-powerful while their victims feel impotent. It can break the human spirit and deeply damage the soul. Someone who used to be strong can become a nervous wreck after a vicious attack. It is not just fear that enters in. Our honor is robbed.

Perhaps your reaction to physical pain was to shut down completely. You created an invisible wall between yourself and the people around you and you lived locked away in your safe place. However, it was lonely and cold behind those closed doors. The Lord wants to heal your heart and lead you out of that emotional prison.

At times, the pain is too much to admit so we toughen up instead. Hurt people inevitably hurt people, and sometimes victims of violence become violent. This can be a male response to the wounds of assault, although it is sometimes true of women too. Anger about being victimized builds inside and the desire to oppress another person can grow.

If you are from a violent background, you may have come to believe that physical brutality is the only way to be heard, or to be strong. It could be that you have lashed out at those you love the most. Maybe you were deeply wounded by someone who was supposed to protect you. You then found yourself becoming like the one who once abused you. The guilt and shame are probably unbearable. The way out is not by beating yourself up. You have already suffered enough. The answer starts with the brave decision to pursue your healing journey.

Control

Joseph must have been broken by the violent attack, but his nightmare was only just beginning. Slavery is degrading. One person owns another human being. All rights are lost. When God created mankind, He told Adam and Eve to have dominion over animals, not over fellow humans. Joseph must have felt like all his dignity had been stripped from him. When one person dominates another, it can destroy their sense of self-worth. You might not have been a slave, but perhaps you have been tightly controlled or intimidated into demonstrating certain behaviors. It may have been a partner or a spouse who was responsible. It could have been a boss who exploited your vulnerability. Perhaps you worked for people who made you feel like your life was meaningless.

Noreen was sent to live with her wealthy aunt in Eastern Nigeria when she was just seven. Her parents were living in desperate poverty and believed that someone else could give her a better future than they could ever offer. Noreen lived with her cousins, but was treated very differently from them. Forced to get up before dawn, she had to clean the house, cook and serve the family.

Her cousins, on the other hand, would wake up to the hearty breakfast she had prepared and then get dressed for school. They would be educated while she would continue scrubbing floors. Leaving her aunt's house aged 16, Noreen eventually found her way to the UK. She married, had children and got a reasonable job. However, her self-esteem was in tatters. She had been squashed. Deep inside, she saw herself as a servant: a little lower than everyone else. She was apologetic, shy and easily intimidated by assertive people.

She was in her 40s when she came to our Healed for Life conference. As the team shared, the scales fell from her eyes. For the first time she understood why she felt the way she did. She believed that she was less important than everyone else. She felt like a doormat. Noreen poured out her pain before the Lord as He revealed the depth of His love for her. She began to realize that, to her Heavenly Father, she was enormously precious. Deep down inside she began to believe that she was wanted. As God healed her heart and drained away years of shame, her view of herself began to change. Now, Noreen is a strong, vibrant wife, mother and minister of the gospel. She sees herself as a highly valuable daughter of the Most High.

Strong Men Cry

Joseph is a great example to us all. Unlike Tamar, he dealt with his pain. He learned to pour out his heart like water in the presence of the Lord. He cried alone, he cried in his father's arms and he even wept with his brothers. Joseph allowed the Lord to heal the pain of that violent attack and the years of being controlled through slavery. He must have given God every sense of sadness and the injustice of false accusation. How do I know that? It is virtually impossible to be kind and generous to the very people who tried to destroy your life unless your heart is healed. He had many years of suffering, but I believe that Joseph learned how to be healed deep down.

Why Can't My Heart Be Healed Instantly?

I once asked the Lord why He usually takes so much time to heal our hearts. I have seen many instant physical miracles. At Healed for Life, while hearts are being restored, we have seen vast numbers of immediate physical healings. Skin diseases have been destroyed, stroke symptoms have vanished, back pain has left, heart conditions have been miraculously resolved, blood diseases have been healed - and all in an instant. However, after many years of ministering to the human heart, I have never seen a soul made whole in a moment. God is clear in His Word that He considers our hearts to be more important than our physical bodies. So I asked the Lord why He appears to heal bodies with more urgency than our hearts. I was blown away by His answer.

The Holy Spirit took me to the second part of Psalm 147:3: "He heals the brokenhearted and binds up their wounds." First, you gently wash a wound. Once it is clean, you softly apply a balm and then you wrap the affected area with a clean bandage. The way God binds up your wounds involves loving care and consideration. Do you remember the kindness that the Good Samaritan showed to the traumatized traveler in Luke 10:25-37? You could safely say that the Samaritan bound up both the man's physical and emotional wounds. The loving care of the stranger in Luke will have been just as healing as the medicine he took.

During the process of being healed, you will experience the tender kindness of your loving Heavenly Father in a life-changing way. Every time you tell the Lord what you went through, and you pour out your pain in His presence, you will experience His incredible healing touch. Each precious encounter will reveal a little more of His love and your true value. Have you ever spent time with someone who is passionate, powerful and important? If for only one moment you are the center of their attention, it can make you feel like you can fly.

Being cherished by the Lord is a thousand times more amazing. Zephaniah 3:17b beautifully expresses His tender loving care for you: "He will rejoice over you with gladness, He will quiet you with His love, He will rejoice over you with singing." During your healing journey, you will experience His warmth and affection like never before. By the time you are whole, you will not only be healed. You will enjoy an indescribable intimacy with the Lord that I don't think you can develop any other way. You will not just have head knowledge of His love. You will know that you are cherished by your Lord.

Your True Confidant

Lamentations 2:19b says, "Pour out your heart like water before the face of the Lord." When you pour out your heart to a close confidant, you tell them secrets you have never before shared. You open up in trust and develop a close bond. Every time you share your deepest issues with God, you open up a new part of your heart to Him. You draw close. Isaiah 9:6 calls Jesus our Wonderful Counselor. The power of counseling is in talking and listening. When we share with the Lord, we meet with our supernatural Counselor who has the power to take all our pain away.

As we say what we never said, it usually releases tears that have been trapped inside. The words are like the cork in a bottle and the pain is similar to the liquid trapped inside. When we tell the Lord what happened and how it made us feel, we will normally weep. It feels so relieving to let the river of pain drain away. Times of healing in His presence are precious to the Lord. Psalms 56:8 (NLT) illustrates the attentiveness of our Heavenly Father: "You keep track of all my sorrows. You have collected all my tears in your bottle. You have recorded each one in your book."

God could heal us in an instant, but instead our Master Restorer heals ours hearts gently, carefully and gradually. It also allows us to get used to the new freedom that comes day by day. He treasures the time that we spend in His presence. He values the incredible closeness we develop on our journey to wholeness. He keeps our tears as a memento of our time together. We come out of the other side both whole and incredibly close to the Lord.

Free at last

Kate was repeatedly raped by her dad from the age of eight. Other male family members soon followed suit. After nine years of relentless sexual abuse, Kate left home, but the damage had been done. Kate's life was a mess. She felt dirty and worthless. She was constantly seeking love yet getting even more wounded.

"I felt like a sex object," she explained. "I was not good enough for anything else except sex." I was weighed down with guilt and very ashamed of myself. I was a warm and friendly girl so I believed the abuse was all my fault. I felt like I was attracting it."

Kate grew up in a church where nobody talked about life's struggles. At the same time, they were constantly reminded that fornication was sin. Kate felt shamed every moment of every day, especially in church. "I felt disgusting," she admitted. "I thought everything about me was horrible."

In 2004, Kate rededicated her life to the Lord and went back to church. Despite every effort to forgive her father, she burned with rage inside. The man that was meant to protect her had stolen her purity. Kate was going round in circles. She reached the place where she longed for real change in her life and relationships. Shame lied to her even though she wanted to believe the truth. "Who am I to think I deserve God's love?" she asked.

When Kate came to Healed for Life, God did more than she imagined possible: "The Lord met with me deep in my heart and lifted pain that had torn my innermost being to pieces. He healed hurts that had defined me. His love was overwhelming." She was delivered from that foul spirit of shame and was healed deep down inside. As she lingered in the presence of God, she heard some words that changed everything: "You are enough; you and God together are enough." For the first time in her life, she felt complete. Kate left feeling a freedom that she did not know existed. She stayed on her healing journey, returning to Healed for Life.

As a result of the depth of healing on the inside, Kate now has a good relationship with her father. She explained: "We talk for hours on the phone. We even reminisce about childhood events. I feel no fear of revisiting old memories. I have no sadness. It feels fantastic to be able to chat with my dad."

It's A Journey

Everyone has a different healing journey. You may already be on your way or you could be taking your first steps. Please remember that it is a journey and it takes time. We are going to pray together soon. You may need to go through this chapter again and again, allowing the Lord to deal with different hurts each time. I encourage you to get hold of my other books. Lifting the Mask and My Whole Heart will be particularly helpful. As God starts to heal you, please stay on your healing journey. As you may have realized from some of the testimonies I have shared, significant inner changes confirm that we are becoming whole. We start to trust, we are not afraid of being hurt and we feel secure.

Isaiah 61:7 (NLT) describes the sweetness of the healing and freedom that await you: "Instead of shame and dishonor, you will enjoy a double share of honor. You will possess a double portion of prosperity in your land, and everlasting joy will be yours." As you surrender, God will turn your life around. We are going to pray. First, we will deal with the pain of being abused. Then we will deal with the hurt of not being helped by those who knew what was going on. We will release forgiveness and, finally, we will tackle shame. Let's pray:

Heavenly Father,

I need to be healed. I have been treated terribly and it broke me inside. I have been hurt, humiliated and abused. I have been betrayed. I ask You to take me on a healing journey. (Now tell the Lord about the first abusive memory that comes to your mind. Tell Him what happened and how you felt. If you were scared, tell the Lord. If you were confused, explain that to God. If they hurt you physically, share that with your Heavenly Father.) It hurt me so badly, Lord. It was not right. It should never have happened. It was not fair. I felt like a piece of trash. It made me feel dirty and stripped of my dignity. Reach into the depths of my heart and heal me, Oh Lord, I pray.

(If people who should have protected you did not help, please pray...)

Lord, that's not all. The people who should have helped me stood by and watched. I felt completely abandoned. They didn't care about me enough to help me. They allowed me to be hurt. It was not fair, and they made it worse. Heal my heart, Oh Lord, I pray. Take away the horrible pain.

(The injustice of abuse is immense. It is therefore very important to your freedom that you forgive those who have hurt you the most. If you are struggling with this, please refer to the chapters on forgiveness in my books Lifting the Mask and 30 Day Detox for your Soul. I would love to now lead you in forgiveness:)

Lord, what they did was unjust, and it was horribly wrong. They used their power to hurt me. I choose today to forgive. I want to be free from the pain of the past and I know that I must therefore forgive. Father, I forgive (now say each of their names) for what they did to me. I release them. I let go of every bit of bitterness and I release them to You. I do not want vengeance. I do not want them to suffer. I let them go and I let what they did go, in Jesus' mighty name.

(Now we will deal with the shame.)

I realize that I have felt ashamed of myself because of what was done to me. I felt dirty, I felt stained. I felt like I had to hide. Lord, I ask that You would now take the foul cloak of shame off my back. I see it being removed right now. Thank You Lord for taking away all shame. Thank You that I was cleansed by the blood of Jesus that was shed on the cross. Thank You that You wash me clean. You make all things new! No stain or blemish can stick to me because You cleanse me of every mark. Thank You that I am washed white as snow. I declare that I am brand new. I am Your precious child. Thank You that You now clothe me with Your honor. I see You wrapping Your robe of righteousness around my shoulders. Thank You, Lord.

I give You all the glory.

In Jesus' name,

Amen.

Chapter 7

GUILT

The weight of guilt is gut-wrenching. It feels like a deep, dark hole without a way out. After all, we are responsible for our mess, so we think we don't deserve a happy ending. Even if no one else knows or cares, we feel judged. We may try to hide our inner conflict, but the tension can be terrible. All too often, we also feel condemned. If a building has been condemned then it is deemed to be unfit for use. We may believe that our actions have disqualified us from the life we once lived or pursued. The guilt is often worsened by regret. You may battle an inner voice that keeps saying: "If only I could turn back the clock and do things differently." However, remorse never changes anything. Even when guilt is hidden, its twin brother shame can still curb our lives.

Ashamed Of Our Errors

After making a complete mess of his life, King David wrote in Psalm 51:3b: "My sin is always before me." It is as though our mistakes stick to us and we cannot wipe the stains away. Messing up can be awful, but it is actually part of life. We are not perfect so you and I will slip up and sin from time to time. The devil attempts to increase the impact of our mistakes by making us feel condemned and ashamed. Proverbs 24:16 makes it clear that falling short is part of life: "For a righteous man may fall seven times and rise again..." You may think that your mistakes make you a disaster, but the Bible tells us that even the righteous fall. And it is not just once a year. Maybe seven times a day! What is important is that we get back up afterwards. That is why shame is such a problem. When we feel disgraced by our sins, we can be tempted to hide or throw in the towel.

Let's look at some sinners in Scripture. Noah got so drunk that he passed out (Genesis 9:21), yet arose the next day to continue in righteousness. Abraham and Isaac both lied about their wives while Jacob cheated his brother out of his birthright. Despite their deceptions, our perfect Lord called Himself: "The God of Abraham, Isaac and Jacob..." (eg Exodus 3:6). David committed adultery and murdered one of his most loyal soldiers. Nonetheless, God called the shepherd king a man after His own heart (Acts 13:22). After three years of walking by the side of our Savior, Peter repeatedly denied that he even knew Jesus. Six weeks later, Peter led more than 3,000 people to salvation in one day (Acts 2:41). John suffered from selfish ambition (see Matthew 20:21) but went on to write books in the Bible which are all about Christian character. These heroes were righteous. They fell and sometimes got into terrible sin. However, they got back up again. They would not allow shame to keep them down.

The Little Box

When he was preaching about forgiveness many years ago, my husband Paul told a story about helping a woman to move. He explained that as they sorted through her belongings, he came across a small metal box. The lady was deeply embarrassed when she saw it. The tin contained cannabis from her days of backsliding. Paul told the story to point out that although this woman had been forgiven and had long since given up cannabis, she was still living under a cloud of shame.

My husband did not say who she was because he knew she still felt ashamed of the discovery. That woman was me. Seeing that tin of dope opened up a cavern of shame in my soul that I would rather have left alone. It took me back to a time when I did many wrong things that I wanted to forget. The experience made me feel dirty and unworthy. It was not the weed I smoked that made me feel bad. It was the dark life that I was living which made me crumple inside.

Romans 6:12 says: "Do not let sin reign." God had completely forgiven me years earlier for every mistake I had made. Nonetheless, sin was still reigning through guilt and shame. Flashbacks from that time made me feel unclean. The thought of people finding out about it made me cringe.

If any memories (however well hidden) still make you squirm, God wants to heal your heart and set you free. When you are forgiven, that is the end of the matter as far as God is concerned. Hebrews 10:17 is clear: "Their sins... I will remember no more." His will is that nothing from your past can condemn you. That way, satan and sin lose their power over you.

Squeaky Clean

Romans 6:6 says, "Knowing this, that our old man was crucified with Him..." This verse set me free. I realized that it wasn't just my sin that Jesus had taken to the cross. Jo the sinner had been crucified with Christ. That woman no longer lived. The person who made mistakes had been put to death with Jesus. Not only had the sin been done away with, but the sinner had been dealt with too! The new me was raised with Christ, clean and forgiven.

It is exactly the same for you. The new you is blameless before God because of Jesus. He wipes away the deliberate iniquities and mistakes of all who are truly sorry. The same blood that is powerful enough to save us is equally able to cleanse us from every error. Isaiah 53:5 explains that Jesus was wounded and crushed for our transgressions and iniquities. A transgression is when I go somewhere I should not go. It is when I do something I should not do. Meanwhile, iniquities are warped and perverted deeds. The word literally means 'the turning of the shoulder'. This is the attitude that says, "I know this is wrong, but I am doing it anyway." Iniquity leads to patterns of bad behavior. They often shroud their victims in shame.

Jesus has already been punished for every one of our mess-ups. He has already made the way for you to be at peace with yourself - and with God. 1 Corinthians 6:11 in the Amplified says: "But you were washed clean (purified by a complete atonement for sin and made free from the guilt of sin), and you were consecrated (set apart, hallowed), and you were justified [pronounced righteous, by trusting] in the name of the Lord Jesus." Once we have confessed to Christ, we are washed completely clean. We don't even smell of sin.

No Place For Shame

It makes no difference what you have done. It might be infidelity, a bad relationship, an addiction to pornography, an outburst, or a lifetime of wrong living. Maybe you agonize over the years that you have wasted, opportunities that you have missed or prayers that you have not prayed. Perhaps you feel that a previous season of promiscuity has stained your reputation with God and man. You might know that you are forgiven, but sense that you must pay the price by living a lesser life.

The Lord died for every mistake you have ever made. Once you say you are sorry and turn aside from wrongdoing, the old passes away and all things become brand new. There is no room for shame or guilt. Before God, you and I are blameless. You have probably heard the explanation of what justification achieves in us. When you trust in the cleansing blood of Jesus to wash you clean, in God's eyes it is just as if you had never sinned. When we are forgiven by Jesus, He looks at us as though we had never messed up in the first place.

The Message version of Psalm 130:3 says: "If you, God, kept records on wrongdoings, who would stand a chance?" None of us would stand a chance if God made us pay for our mistakes. Your faults are no different to mine. I am cleansed today of impatience or pride in the same way that I was made new decades ago after years of impurity.

When my children were small and they had an argument, I sent one upstairs and told the other to stay downstairs. I separated them. The Bible says that God separates you from your sin 'as far as the east is from the west' (Psalm 103:12). After you ask God to forgive you, He removes your wrongdoing from you. It is no longer yours. It has gone. Isaiah 53:5b says, "The chastisement for our peace was upon Him..." Chastisement means punishment. He was punished for every mess you and I have ever made. He does not want you to feel ashamed of your mistakes. He wants you to enjoy being clean in Christ. He longs for you to know the boldness that an innocent man or woman freely enjoys.

Abortion

Several years ago, God gave me a word of knowledge for a woman at a conference. He told me that this precious lady was bound with guilt and grief about an abortion several years earlier. I had shared the story that day of my daughter's tragic death. The Lord gave me a very clear instruction about how to address this woman. I told her, "You and I are the same. We are both grieving mothers." She broke down and sobbed. For the first time in her life, she felt she had permission to grieve over her loss. The Holy Spirit reached into the depths of her heart and brought powerful healing. After that, we dealt with the shame. She suddenly understood deep down that Jesus had paid the price for her mistakes. The shame melted away and we dedicated her little one to our Father's care in heaven.

Buried Guilt

Cate and Greg met at university. Cate was backslidden and Greg was not yet born again. They began a sexual relationship. Towards the end of their studies, God gloriously saved Greg and Cate rededicated her life to Jesus. However, they struggled with purity. While they were trying to get back on track, Cate's pastor came to see her. They spent some wonderful time together. Before she left, Cate's leader asked about the young couple's purity. Too embarrassed to admit the truth, Cate lied: "We are great. No sex before marriage for us!"

The couple grew strong, won their battle and abstained until their wedding. Soon after they were married, Cate started to struggle with sex. She felt dirty every time she was intimate with Greg. She would be disgusted at herself but had no idea why she felt so awful. At times, she pushed her husband away. About a year into the marriage, Cate attended one of our conferences. I talked about Rebekah's Request.

Why Am I Like This?

The Bible characters Isaac and Rebekah had been believing for a baby for a long time. After twenty years of persistent prayer,

Rebekah conceived. As the pregnancy developed, something did not feel quite right. We do not know whether Rebekah was in pain or if she was just churning inside. Whatever it was, she prayed a powerful prayer which we refer to as 'Rebekah's Request'. In Genesis 25:22, Rebekah came to the Lord and asked, "If all is well then why am I like this?" God told her that she was carrying twins!

Rebekah's Request can help you and I in all sorts of situations. If you overreact to life's normal ups and downs, it's a great prayer to pray. If you get upset when people forget your birthday or make you the butt of their jokes, it is a helpful question to ask God. I prayed that prayer on a regular basis during my season of intense healing. It is amazing how many of our regular reactions are actually the result of unhealed hurts. If you ask the Lord to reveal the heart causes for any of your behaviors, He will answer. It is better to deal with any underlying issues in your heart than to treat the symptoms.

Cate prayed: "If all is well, then why do I feel so bad about having sex with my husband?" The Holy Spirit shone His light into Cate's heart and showed her that she was battling with the guilt of her premarital sexual relationship. She had struggled to shake off the feeling of sin. God had forgiven her, but she was still ashamed of herself. Because she felt unclean, she was seeing sex as dirty. Cate poured out her heart like water in the presence of the Lord and the shame melted away. She went home transformed and began to enjoy marital intimacy.

Any Time Sex Was Mentioned...

There was one issue that remained. Any time sex was mentioned in church, Cate would cringe with embarrassment. After ten years of marriage, Cate - who was now a leader - was asked to join three other speakers and participate in a question and answer panel at a ladies' conference. Several questions about sex were put to the panel. While others answered openly, Cate visibly squirmed her way through the session.

Once again, Cate used Rebekah's Request to enquire of the Lord: "If all is well, then why am I like this?" (Genesis 25:19). God answered. He showed her that she still carried shame about lying to her leader all those years earlier. At the end of the session, she spoke to her pastor and apologized for hiding the truth. Instantly, ten years of shame were lifted from her. No prayer was even needed. The light of the truth broke its power. John 8:44 exposes the devil's nature: "...He is a liar and the father of lies." If you have been believing the lie that your mistakes disqualify you, please let the Lord set you free today.

Pornography

Shame thrives in the shadows. It feeds on its victims' fears of exposure. Secrecy increases the grip that pornography holds in its victims' lives. It makes people feel dirty and unworthy. For many, this is a carefully hidden addiction that you have never shared with even your nearest or dearest. The devil preys upon you, pushing you further into this dark, lonely world, and then he plagues you afterwards with unbearable guilt. It's like having a friend who pressurizes you into shoplifting from a local store, and then guilt-trips you for stealing for the rest of the week. It is a dark and difficult place. However, the same Jesus who died to save your soul also paid the price for your freedom from pornography. God is bigger than the things that are bigger than you. Shame will try to keep you sin-conscious, constantly thinking about what you have done wrong. The Lord wants you to dwell on His power to bring forgiveness and freedom. The blood of Jesus makes you completely clean. When guilt and shame are broken, you will be able to set your faith on total freedom.

Disarming Secrets

Our Savior is the God of Truth, whereas the devil is the father of lies. I have witnessed many being set free simply by bringing their hidden baggage into the light. I encourage you to ask yourself a question. Are there secrets in the corridors of your soul that you work hard to keep hidden? Do you have any memories that you fear might be exposed one day? It is the enemy who wants us to keep the past locked away behind closed doors.

I am not suggesting that we should broadcast our failures. Neither should we be embarrassed about any season of our life that has been forgiven and forgotten by Jesus. 1 John 1:9 says, "If we confess our sins, He is faithful and just to forgive us our sins and to cleanse us from all unrighteousness." As soon as we repent, He forgives, and sin loses its power. The only way that satan can keep his grip on confessed sin is through our unresolved guilt or lingering shame.

Growing Up

My daughter Abby has always been conscientious. When she was in elementary school, she used to feel terrible any time she got something wrong. If she had done a math or spelling test, she would be unduly upset by her mistakes. One day she came home excited because she had gotten everything right. I asked her what she had learned as a result of that exam. She was puzzled so I repeated the question. Eventually she replied, "Well I didn't learn anything, Mummy, because I already knew it all." I followed that up with another question. "What did you learn last week when you got some answers wrong?" Abby suddenly realized that she learned more when she made mistakes. It took a while, but Abby ended up understanding the value of getting things wrong. She no longer felt bad when she failed. My little girl learned early that her errors could help her grow.

There is no doubt that we learn more in the valleys of our lives than on the mountaintops. My husband recently preached the best message I have ever heard about repentance. He explained the meaning of the word in the Greek. Metanoeō translated as repent literally means to think differently or afterwards. It is the ability to look back and evaluate. Real repentance is not just about weeping and wailing. 2 Corinthians 7:10 tells us that sadness about sin is helpful if it creates change in behavior: "For godly sorrow produces repentance..." Notice that godly sorrow is not repentance, but it can bring us to repentance.

Beating myself up for missing the mark will not help me to become a better person. That is how shame wants me to react. Looking back at my behavior and deciding how I could do things differently is what enables me to grow. Have you made some serious mistakes that have left you feeling like a failure? Maybe you believe that you messed up one time too many. Perhaps you have hurt someone very special. Let me remind you, God is bigger than the things that are bigger than you. That is what makes Him God.

It Started In The Garden

There is something about sinning that makes us feel uncovered. Shame was the first fallen feeling. After mankind's first ever sin, Adam and Eve experienced the sense of nakedness. They felt exposed and embarrassed. They will have had some pleasure for a moment, but they soon felt stripped by their own actions. Maybe that is how you feel: uncovered. Although we are tempted in the moment by sin's seduction, the short term gain it offers is always followed by longer term pain. Speaking of Adam and Eve, Genesis 3:7 says, "...they knew that they were naked; and they sewed fig leaves together and made themselves coverings." The sense of exposure that sin brings often makes us want to cover up or look away. Facing our failures can be intensely uncomfortable.

Shame might also make us want to run away. Adam and Eve tried to hide themselves from the Lord. They could not bear the burden of guilt and could not handle their moral failure. Let me stop for a minute. If you have missed the mark, the enemy may be telling you it is over. He could be trying to convince you that you have no way out. That is a lie. Please do not run away from your Heavenly Father. Run to Him. He has a plan for your redemption.

Contingency Planning

All responsible major companies use what is called contingency planning. Senior management teams periodically rehearse procedures to address this question: what will we do if things go wrong? Protocols are put in place to ensure organizations can recover in the event of major mistakes or unforeseen problems. The vast majority of companies will have had to employ these plans at one time or another. Matthew 7:11 says, "If you sinful people know how to give good gifts to your children, how much more will your heavenly Father give good gifts to those who ask him." If secular leaders know how to get their companies back on track after a crisis, don't you think God knows how to redirect your life after a difficulty or diversion?

The famous verse in Jeremiah 29:11 (NIV) says, "'For I know the plans I have for you," declares the Lord, "plans to prosper you and not to harm you, plans to give you hope and a future.'"

It does not say 'plan', implying that there is just one option. It says 'plans' because the Lord has a whole host of contingencies! Do you feel like you have blown it? Perhaps a critical decision has left you on the wrong track. Maybe you fear that you have missed God's purposes for your life. It could be the result of your own or other people's decisions.

I want you to know that God is the greatest at pulling us back into His purposes. Romans 8:28 (NLT) says, "And we know that God causes everything to work together for the good of those who love God and are called according to his purpose for them." No matter what has happened, God is able to reroute your life for your good.

Remember, when the Lord restores, He makes things even better than they were. The Lord's Plan B (or even C!) is far beyond what you could ask for or imagine. When I look back over my life, I have made a catalogue of mistakes and yet each time I fell or failed, God turned it around for my good and for the benefit of others. All you need to do is surrender again. Entrust your heart and life into His hands and believe that He has the best in store for you. I do not know how He does it, but our God makes a way where there seems to be no way.

Public Guilt

Ruby was a worship leader at her church. She had protected her purity since her youth, keeping herself for the man she would marry. When she was in her early thirties, a womanizer relentlessly pursued her. She lost her virginity and conceived all in one night. Devastated, she determined to leave her church and city without telling a soul. Ruby could not handle the thought of telling her pastors. They had believed in her gift and raised her up into leadership, and now she had let them down. She planned to pack her things and move. Certain that she had missed God's purpose for her life, Ruby was ready to run away.

God supernaturally brought her pregnancy to her pastor's attention. He drove to her house, picked her up and took Ruby back to his family's home. There were plenty of tears, but then they put together a plan. Ruby was stepped down from leadership, the church was told, and Ruby and her newborn baby moved in with the pastors. When her precious little girl was about one, Ruby resumed leading worship and was eventually promoted to head up the praise department. It looked like all was well. Her life was back on track. However, shame still crippled this woman. She dearly loved her daughter but felt deep disgrace about being a single mother. Ruby worried that everyone knew her sordid story. Although she realized she was forgiven, she still felt marked by her mistakes.

Several years later, Ruby came to Healed for Life. We were ministering from Psalms 8:3-5. Scripture says that the Lord is mindful of you and me. He thinks about us. It goes on to say that He crowns us with His glory and clothes us with His honor. The Lord understands our humanity and vulnerability, so He covers us with His honor. He clothes us with His dignity. As Ruby listened, the words pierced her heart. She broke down and wept. The shame that had clung to her for years was exposed to the light of God's love and its power broke. The Holy Spirit reached into the depths of Ruby's heart and healed her of every sense of disgrace. She left with her head held high, knowing she was an honorable woman. Soon after the shame lifted, Ruby met her husband. The plans the Lord had for her proved to be awesome.

It Makes Supernatural Sense

My second real job was working for a top public relations company. I moved from Manchester in the north west of England to London to take up my new role. I was doing very well, and the future looked bright. One morning when I was praying, I sensed God clearly calling me into full-time ministry. The pull was strong. Not long after that, I was offered the opportunity of running a three-month project at my church. I remember the day that I handed in my notice like it was yesterday. I was giving up a hugely promising career to take up a short-term, part-time position. My new weekly salary barely covered my rent, never mind my living expenses.

I was fasting the day I told my boss and I went to a cafe straight after giving him my notice. I ordered a drink and pulled out my Bible. As I was reading, a complete stranger came up to me with a word from the Lord: "God is saying that He is with you. The things of the Spirit are like swimming," she continued. "Whether you are an inch out of your depth or a mile, it is the same substance holding you up." It might sound like a strange word to you, but it made perfect sense to me. Trusting God for my rent would be no different from trusting Him for favor at work. Now turn this principle around. The same blood that wiped away your sins at salvation can erase every major (and minor) mess in your life. You just need to believe in the infinite power of that blood.

How Do We React?

After King David committed adultery and murder, he looked his horrific sin in the face, held up his hands and confessed. He fell headlong into the mercy of God and the Lord led him forwards. He had faith in our Heavenly Father. In Psalms 51:7, he cried out, "Purge me with hyssop, and I shall be clean; wash me, and I shall be whiter than snow." He focused on God's faithfulness, not his terrible sins. He believed in the supernatural power of the Lord to cleanse him from sin. David rose out of shame and back into the goodness of God. Saul, in contrast, tried to cover his shortcomings and made excuses for his mistakes. His sins were nowhere near as dramatic as David's. Saul did not commit adultery and he did not kill. However, he would not take responsibility for his failings. He did what shame often tries to get its victims to do. He covered up his mistakes and blamed everyone but himself.

The Blame Game

Shame is so vile that we do not want to accept its mark on our life. As we have already said, under its influence we sometimes hide. At other times we lash out in anger. Another reaction to this foul feeling is to blame. Right from the start, we see this human response to humiliation. When God asked Adam in the Garden of Eden if he had eaten the forbidden fruit, he said: "The woman whom You gave to be with me, she gave me of the tree, and I ate." (Genesis 3:12). Adam could not bear to accept responsibility. It probably made him feel dreadful. Instead, he pointed the finger at his wife, and even at God for giving her to him. Eve was a quick learner and soon followed suit: 'And the Lord God said to the woman, "What is this you have done?" The woman said, "The serpent deceived me, and I ate."' (Genesis 3:13)

Blame is another way that we divert our attention from the real issues. It takes our eyes off our pain and onto someone else's problems. Blame does not take shame away. It only temporarily distracts us from its pain. One of the hardest things to do is to look shame in the face. It is also one of the most liberating experiences. When we are afraid to look back, the events of the past retain power. When we make the decision to face each painful picture, they start to lose their grip over our lives.

If you have any memories that make you want to turn away, they are memories that God still needs to heal. If you have any recollections that cause you to recoil, the Lord wants to do a deep work within. We need to reach the place where we can look at every inner picture of our past without any pain or shame. That is when the enemy is stripped of his power over us. We are going to deal with these issues in prayer, but first let's look at how we get the last laugh...

The Turnaround

Jesus forgives, but that is not all. He gives us a fresh start and even improves our lives. He wipes away the mistakes of the past and then enhances the future. He gives you a double portion of God's goodness for every mistake. Isaiah 61:7 says, "Instead of your shame, you shall have double honor..." Jesus wipes away all our shame and cleanses us deep within. He then gives us double honor. How do you honor someone? You respect them, you treat them like a VIP and you celebrate them. The Lord clothes you with honor to show you that a new day has dawned. This is one of the ways that the Lord rubs the devil's nose in his defeat. He blesses us all the more. That is the amazing mercy of God. Let's pray.

Heavenly Father,

I realize that I am carrying guilt and shame for things I have done wrong. When I remember my mistakes, I feel a sense of disgrace. I don't like looking back at certain events in my life. I don't want to carry the weight of guilt or the pain of shame any longer.

Father, I thank You that You forgave me of every wrong I ever committed the moment I confessed. Thank You that You separated me from my sin as far as the east is from the west. Thank You that the blood of Jesus washed me completely clean. I am brand new. It is not only my sin that was nailed to the cross, but the sinner who was crucified with Christ. The old me that did those things was crucified with Christ. The new me has been acquitted. I am the righteousness of God in Christ Jesus.

I am fed up of feeling ashamed. I felt disgraced by sin that You had already forgiven. Thank You, Lord, that you dealt with my shame when you paid for my sins. I break the power of shame over my life. I declare that I am clean, and I am free. The blood of Jesus has washed me as white as snow.

Not only that. When shame tries to raise its ugly head, please remind me to use Rebekah's Request. Help me to remember to ask You to bring hidden issues to the surface so that I can be cleansed and healed.

I now receive Your double honor. I see You covering me with Your robe of righteousness and placing a crown of glory on my head. Thank You, Lord, that I am Your child which makes me royalty.

I give all You all the glory.

In Jesus' name,

Amen.

Chapter 8

SHATTERED DREAMS

The big day was just three weeks away. Lara's lifelong dreams were about to come true. Then the call came. "It's Phil. I can't do this. I don't want to marry you. I'm sorry. It's over." In a one-minute conversation, Lara's world fell apart. Every expectation of her happily-ever-after was smashed to bits. Her mum spent the next few days canceling every arrangement and telling friends and family the awful news. Lara was broken-hearted. She also felt publicly humiliated. Some people pretended not to know, while others offered patronizing pity. Everything inside Lara wanted to crawl away and hide.

Your story may not be as dramatic or public as Lara's. That does not necessarily lessen the pain. Perhaps you were passed over for a long-awaited promotion. Maybe you have been believing for healing but you're still sick. It could be that your dreams have been dashed. We all experience disappointment. Although we know it hurts, we think it is harmless. However, disappointment can be dangerous. All too often, we feel like putting our lives on hold or giving up on our dreams. It can dent our faith for the future.

Disappointment is a mix of sadness and a sense of injustice. Sadness is obvious. We have been hoping and believing for something to happen and then there is nothing. We feel hurt that our hopes do not materialize. The sense of injustice comes from the fact that we did not get what we expected. Perhaps your faith was high. Maybe you were fully believing that you would receive. When we have our sights firmly fixed on breakthrough and then it all crashes down around us, it can make us feel let down.

A Fool

There is another side to disappointment. When we have shared our hopes with friends and family, we can feel like a fool when our dreams fade away. It can seem like we are being stripped in public. Sympathetic smiles on the faces of onlookers can be horribly patronizing. The bigger the ambition, the greater the fall. It is made worse when we felt certain that we would enjoy a positive outcome. Thankfully, Lara came out the other side. She attended one of our conferences and God healed her heart. He removed every sense of disgrace. Lara left with her head held high, knowing her immense value.

Inner humiliation can be worsened by mockery from the people around us. Psalm 69:20 in the Message sums up how it can feel. "I'm broken by their taunts, flat on my face, reduced to a nothing..." Even when people are not making insensitive comments, sometimes we hear them as though they are. Perhaps you told the world that your new business would take off and instead it was a big flop. Maybe you fought hard for a promotion at work, but the job was offered to your co-worker who has now become your boss. Maybe you were given a wonderful new opportunity. You shared your delight with friends. Then the manager who made you the offer changed their mind.

Jeremiah 3:25 says, "We lie down in our shame, and our reproach covers us..." When we lie down, we give up. Reproach means disgrace. When we have shared our dreams, disappointment can make us feel disgraced. This verse says it covers us. These might seem like insignificant issues. No one has died. There is still food on the table. The problem is that for you and I to fulfill our purpose, we need to pursue our God-given dreams with great determination. James 1:15 tells us that desire gives birth. When we long for something to happen, it creates the motivation we need to get the job done. When our hopes are dashed, it can quench our desire and cause us to give up. That's why we need to deal with these issues. Your destiny may well depend on it.

My 'Big' Breakthrough

After years of prayer, one of my books - 30 Day Detox for your Soul - was picked up by a US publishing house. God supernaturally arranged the whole thing. By divine chance, the company's Pittsburgh-based chief executive visited my church in London and attended a conference we were hosting. By the end of day one, the deal was sealed! Naturally, I assumed that everything else would take off like a rocket.

The publishers told me that their main aim would be to get me onto Sid Roth's show, 'It's Supernatural!' They felt certain he would like the book (and my British accent!). I rallied together a team of warriors who took the matter up in prayer. I had many prophetic words and scriptural promises that became the basis of our intercession. Our office printed bookmarks showing our goals and distributed them to our prayer team. Around that time, I met several folk who had close connections with Sid or his producers. Everything was heading in the right direction.

Just as I landed in Denmark to speak at a conference, I got a call from my publisher. "Sid's people love your book and they love you!" I was thrilled. As soon as I hung up, I called my husband with the great news. Then I texted our prayer team leader.

Everyone was excited. During the meetings in Denmark, I shared the story of praying and believing. I explained that the wait had been tough, but the outcome was glorious. After a packed weekend, I headed home with a happy heart.

An Unfortunate Misunderstanding

A week later, I received an email from my publicist: "I do apologize. There was an unfortunate misunderstanding. My boss and I had crossed wires. The show does not want to feature your book." It was like a punch in the guts. I now had to go back to all the people who had celebrated the success and put them straight. I felt bad for the intercessors who had assumed their prayers had been answered. I was embarrassed that I had celebrated and felt like a fool. It wasn't even as though some other big television network had snapped me up. Apart from some smaller shows, the book did not get much media coverage. I felt like a fraud and I felt stupid to have believed in the first place.

Let me stop for a moment. Remember, the enemy has a purpose for your pain. Satan wants to exploit every ounce of embarrassment that you feel. He wants you to dismiss your dreams as childish or misguided. The devil wants you to walk away from the hopes that once mattered so much. Even when we know deep inside that we were destined to accomplish certain things, disappointment can make us want to throw in the towel.

The embarrassment of disappointment is no different from other forms of shame. It feels uncomfortable so it is hard to admit. One of the ways you will know if you have dealt with a matter is by asking yourself how you feel when you look back. Lamentations 3:20 describes how unhealed memories affect us: "My soul still remembers and sinks within me." If thinking about certain experiences still causes a churning on the inside, you probably need to be healed.

Over the next few years, at least four different friends in ministry told me that they would help me get a book on a big show. Over and over again, their efforts failed, and my hopes evaporated. I reached the place where I didn't want to hear the names of certain TV show hosts because they reminded me of my defeats. I wanted to shrink back. Eventually, I got into the presence of God about this issue. "I'm fed up, Lord. I would rather give up. I feel stupid for trying. Wash away all the embarrassment, I pray." I left His presence healed and free to believe again.

The So-Called Father Of Faith

Imagine how Abraham must have felt. He and Sarah lived at a time in history when names were given because of their meaning. God gave Abraham his name because it means father of multitudes. The Lord told him that he would have a son, but he had to wait 25 years for this promise to come to pass. He must have felt so stupid introducing himself to new people. "Hi. I'm an old man with no children, but I'm the Father of Multitudes!" I'm sure shame knocked at his door as decades passed without any sign of Sarah getting pregnant. He must have had to push past people's opinions and deal with all his disappointments.

It is vital that we understand Romans 10:10: "With the heart one believes..." Faith lives and grows in your heart, not your head. It is therefore hard to believe God while you are weighed down with discouragement. It will be important to deal with your disappointments so that you can get back up and build your faith again.

Romans 4:18 (NLT) says, "Even when there was no reason for hope, Abraham kept hoping-believing that he would become the father of many nations. For God had said to him, 'That's how many descendants you will have.'" He hoped even when he ran out of hope. That is much easier to do when your heart is healed.

We need to tackle every issue that the enemy uses against us. Dealing with disappointment - and the various problems it produces - is vital. I have already mentioned the sadness, injustice and shame it produces. There are other important reasons why we need to drive it out of our lives.

1. Dead Weight

Disappointment sits like a rock in our souls. It does not usually dissolve over time. More often than not, it increases. We may have been let down at work, and then something happens at home. Although these might be isolated incidents, they can create a sense that everything is falling apart around us. No longer is there just one rock sitting in our souls. Now there are several weighing us down. Sadness opens the door to the spirit of heaviness.

Heaviness of heart is terrible. It is a sinking sadness. It feels as if a blanket is covering your soul. It can make God's people feel despondent. When we are heavy-hearted, we find ourselves thinking thoughts we would not otherwise consider. We might think: "This is too much." Or: "I feel like giving up." Maybe we say to ourselves: "I've had enough of all this." In Psalm 119:28, King David said, "My soul melts from heaviness." This verse shows that the devil intends to use that weight on the inside to cause you to melt. He wants you to be weak and weary. Ultimately, he wants you to give up. If we have had several let-downs, each one weighs us down just a little bit more. Left unchecked, the heaviness can lead to depression.

Heaven's Prescription

Some time ago, I was very heavy-hearted. I had experienced an intense few weeks packed with difficult family challenges. I was feeling down. That opened the door for the spirit of heaviness and thoughts of despondency. I prayed and worshipped, but nothing shifted. I even asked God to send someone to encourage me. I was fed up and felt like giving up. I cried out to God for help. Almost immediately, I was taken straight to Isaiah 61:3b which describes the antidote to heaviness: "... The garment of praise for the spirit of heaviness..." I knew what I had to do. I did not feel like praising. The book of Hebrews calls it the sacrifice of praise! We don't praise because we feel like singing. We praise because it is the right thing to do. We praise because He is worthy. And we praise because it is heaven's prescription for heaviness!

I was out shopping when God told me to praise. I did not care who was watching. I just started to declare: "There is no one like our God. I will praise Him, praise Him..." Within seconds - yes, just a matter of seconds - the heaviness that had been hanging around for several days lifted. If you're heavy-hearted, don't delay. Start to praise and continue to praise until every last weight has lifted. Once the heaviness has gone, we can deal with the underlying disappointment.

2. Downbeat

Disappointment opens the door to discouragement, which makes us feel like throwing in the towel. Discouragement is one of the devil's trusted weapons to "wear out the saints" (Daniel 7:25). The enemy wants to make God's people slow down or even give up. While we must pour out disappointment, we must kick out discouragement. I will lead you in prayer at the end of this section. We need to treat each symptom with the appropriate action. At Ziklag, King David went through probably the greatest setback of his life. We read the account in 1 Samuel 30 of the king returning from a thwarted battle effort to find his family gone, and his home and city burned to the ground. He was brokenhearted.

First, King David poured out his heart before the Lord: "David and the people who were with him lifted up their voices and wept, until they had no more power to weep." (1 Samuel 30:4). He poured out the pain of disappointment. Second, he picked himself up and reminded himself of the goodness and faithfulness of God: "... David encouraged and strengthened himself in the Lord his God." (1 Samuel 30:6b Amplified). King David kicked out discouragement.

3. Derailment

Faith is the currency of the kingdom and the only way we can accomplish God's plans for our lives. Hebrews 11:1 explains where faith comes from: "Faith is the substance of things hoped for...". Just as water makes ice, so hope produces faith. Without water, we cannot produce ice. Without hope, we will never be able to grow our faith. Just as oil and water cannot mix, so disappointment and hope cannot coexist. If we don't deal with disappointment in the deep recesses of our souls, it will stifle hope and faith in our lives. Then the shame of dashed dreams can all too easily cause us to hide. We need to drive it all out of our lives.

Getting Free

Maybe by now, you're realizing that you're carrying a muddy mix of emotions about delayed or dashed dreams. One of the things that makes disappointment so painful is that very often our faith was involved. We believed, but we were let down. Sometimes we feel upset with God. At other times we think God is upset with us. Either way, we don't think we can tell the Lord how we really feel. That is not true. Psalm 139:2 tells us that He knows our thoughts. He understands what is going on inside you and He wants to help you find your way out. Even if you are angry with Him, our Heavenly Father can handle the truth! After all, He is the God of truth. In fact, He desires truth in the inward parts (Psalm 51:6).

If you will be honest with God and tell Him what happened (or didn't happen) and exactly how it all made you feel, He will heal your heart and cleanse every ounce of shame. He takes the sting out of awkward memories so that we can look back without any discomfort. He does this when we bring it all into the light of His healing presence.

Letting God

It doesn't stop there. Once you have shared your sadness and poured out your pain, He wants you to leave your disappointment with Him. This is how we deal with the injustice of disappointment. We let it go! We lay down the feeling that we have been let down. We give it to God as an offering. We bring it to the Lord as a sacrifice. When your heart is free of the pain and shame of disappointment, you will be ready to dream and believe again.

Heavenly Father,

I am disappointed. I realize that I have been carrying rocks around in my soul and I am weighed down. I felt like a fool for believing in the first place. I shared my dreams and then they got dashed. (Now tell the Lord exactly what happened and how it made you feel. If you felt disgraced or embarrassed, tell the Lord. Explain how the whole thing affected you. If you are carrying several disappointments, you will need to pour out the pain and shame of each one.) Heal my heart deep down inside, Oh Lord, and take away every sense of shame.

Now I make a decision. I lay down the disappointment as an offering. I give You every sense of injustice. I lay down every letdown. I let it go. I give it all to You as an offering. It's now Yours. It is not mine.

I take my eyes off what happened, and I look to You, Oh Lord. I put my trust in You again. I put my hope in You, Oh Lord. Thank You that the plans You have for me are to prosper me and not to harm me. Your plans for my life are good and my future is bright.

I give You all the praise and glory.

In Jesus' name,

Amen.

Chapter 9

THE WAY I AM

Many women wear wigs to give themselves a new look. Maria wore one to cover her baldness. Once, she was proud of her beautiful brown mane, but this precious lady's hair fell out during a season of serious financial stress. Although she came to terms with the situation, it was rare for Maria to allow anyone to see her bare head. Even at night, she wore a cap to stop her husband from looking at it.

One wet and windy day, Maria went to pick up her children from elementary school. Just as pupils poured out of the gates, the breeze picked up. A sudden gust lifted Maria's wig right off her head and deposited it on the ground ahead of her. Running desperately to grab her hairpiece, she reached the spot only for another gust to sweep it still further away. The wind was playing a cruel round of 'you can't catch me'! Eventually, another mom sprinted ahead and snatched the wig out of the wind's grip. Maria grabbed it, covered her head, took her children by the hands and ran. She was devastated. Not only had she provided a ridiculous spectacle for every onlooker, she had exposed her shiny scalp for all to see. All this was in front of her children and their friends.

Harrowing Yet Revealing

Once home, Maria called her pastor who was also a close friend. She sobbed as she recounted her story of humiliation. She poured out her heart like water as she shared her shame. The Holy Spirit reached into the depths of her being and healed her heart. He relieved the pain of the moment, but He also dealt with buried shame. At the time of writing, Maria is still believing for her hair to grow back. While waiting, she is neither ashamed nor insecure about her appearance. In fact, as Maria is a powerful preacher, removing her wig has become a fairly frequent sermon illustration!

Unpleasant experiences can often expose the true state of our souls. When all is well, it can be easy to assume that we are perfectly secure. Pressure squeezes out the truth. Why would a bold, beautiful believer be painfully embarrassed about being bald? Underlying issues made this experience more unpleasant. In Psalm 139:14, King David declared, "I will praise You, for I am fearfully and wonderfully made; marvelous are Your works, and that my soul knows very well." It does not say that you and I are perfect. It says that you are marvelous just the way you are. One sign of inner well-being is when we know deep inside that we are pleasing, despite any defects. There is no spot or blemish, no flaw or failing, that has the right to make you feel inferior. You are made in the wonderful image of God. If you dislike any aspect of your physical appearance, God wants to repair your view of yourself.

Crippled

Mephibosheth was Jonathan's son and King Saul's grandson. He is introduced to us in 2 Samuel 4:4. At the tender age of five, Mephibosheth had a terrible, life-altering accident. His carer was hurrying to flee enemy armies after Jonathan and Saul were killed in battle. The nurse picked up the little boy but dropped him as she ran. The fall must have been horrendous because Mephibosheth permanently damaged his feet, leaving him lame.

It is amazing how hurtful human reactions can be. It is common for people to stare at scars, glare at difference and be repulsed by deformity. When that happens, we often decide that our physical features make us inferior. Perhaps you think you are too short or too tall. Maybe you try to hide that birthmark. It could be that you are very self-conscious about your ears, your nose or legs. Do you feel fat or even ugly?

God wants to restore your view of yourself from the inside out. Proverbs 23:7 says, "As a man thinks in his heart, so is he..." He wants to heal your heart of every hurtful memory. The Lord wants to strip away every shred of self-hatred. When you understand that your value is based on your immense worth to God, you will be able to appreciate your unique physical form. I have watched the countenances of men and women completely change at Healed for Life as their hearts were restored.

Dead Dog

Growing up in a society that looked down on disabled people, Mephibosheth soon saw himself as a second-class citizen. This is a problem. When we think we are less valuable than other people, we won't believe that we deserve the blessings of God. We can end up closing the very doors that God is opening. Proverbs 23:18 says that the expectation of the righteous will not be cut off. Put differently, we get what we expect. When we think we are worthless, we don't believe we deserve much.

Years later, King David was looking for someone that he could bless for the sake of his late friend, Jonathan. Mephibosheth was brought before the king. "So David said to him, 'Do not fear, for I will surely show you kindness for Jonathan your father's sake, and will restore to you all the land of Saul your grandfather; and you shall eat bread at my table continually.'" 2 Samuel 9:7)

Are You Ready For Your Big Break?

This was Mephibosheth's big break! Probably like you and me, Mephibosheth had been praying for change. He was offered all the land that once belonged to his grandfather, King Saul. This was a huge opportunity. However, Mephibosheth did not believe he deserved such abundant blessings. Listen to his response: "Then he bowed himself, and said, 'What is your servant, that you should look upon such a dead dog as I?'" (2 Samuel 9:8). He saw himself as a nobody, so he shunned the goodness of God. Shame makes us turn away and hide. It hates the spotlight and runs away from lavish love. Opportunity knocked, but Mephibosheth was not ready for his destiny.

Too Small

One of the most significant words I have ever received was spoken over me at Bible college. I can't remember the topic being taught that day or why I had gone to the front of the auditorium for prayer. However, I will never forget what the Dean of Students pronounced as he prayed over me: "You're too small! You're too small in your own eyes." I can still hear those words like it was yesterday.

You know the story of the twelve spies. Their job was to glean information about Canaan and report back to Moses. Remember, God had sworn that He would give them the land. He performed miracle after miracle delivering the Jewish people from Pharaoh and then providing for them in the desert. They knew from experience that God was both faithful and able. For God to use us, we must believe in Him. But we must also believe in ourselves. Ten of the twelve spies did not believe that they were able. Listen to their assessment of the situation...

"The land through which we have gone as spies is a land that devours its inhabitants, and all the people whom we saw in it are men of great stature. There we saw the giants... and we were like grasshoppers in our own sight..." (Numbers 13:32-33). They saw themselves like insignificant insects. When we have a diminished view of ourselves, all too often we will have an inflated opinion of others. The spies first saw the inhabitants of the land as 'men of great stature' and soon convinced themselves that they were 'giants'. The smaller we feel, the bigger we believe others are. For example, I might be going for a job interview and start worrying that the other candidates are better qualified than me. Before long, I may end up imagining that they can walk on water!

Your Projector

Your view of yourself will be eroded if you struggle with shame. When we have a poor self-image, it affects the way we carry ourselves and the opinions that others have of us too. The verse about the spies goes on to say that because the ten leaders saw themselves as insignificant insects, the inhabitants of the land saw them that way too: "And so we were in their sight." Numbers 13:33b. Your self-image is like a projector. It conveys who you are to others. Proverbs 23:7 says: "As a man thinks in his heart so is the man."

The spies were supposed to be invading a foreign land, but they believed their enemies were stronger than they were. They lost hope and caved in to fear. I doubt that invading a nation is on your agenda. Nonetheless, whether it is a business venture, a marriage proposal or a new ministry, your view of yourself will affect how you appear to others and how they respond to you.

Every word in the Bible is there for a purpose. Mephibosheth means dispeller of shame. This young man was born with a mandate to banish shame from his own life and the lives of others. He was called to confront and conquer this enemy. I do not believe he ever really arose and shook off shame. Why don't you decide that you will pick up his mantle as one who dispels shame? As you face the issues that have dragged you down and allow the Lord to bring healing, you will arise strong. When shame has been eliminated, it will be easier to pursue your unique purpose.

Marked By Mockery

Heidi is a passionate youth pastor who came to Healed for Life. She did not think she needed healing and only signed up because her pastor encouraged her. We are often unaware of the issues hiding in our hearts. That is why Jeremiah 17:9 says, "The heart is deceitful above all things... Who can know it?" We do not know how much pain is buried deep down which hampers our lives. Heidi was no different.

She recalled: "During one of the sessions, God took me back to a long-forgotten childhood memory that I never realized had marked my entire life. I came to the UK from Africa when I was just five years old. My English was not great. One day at school, a group of children teased me about the way I spoke. I retaliated in my thick African accent, 'Stop harassing me!' That was a red rag to a bull. They burst into fits of giggles, imitating and mocking me. I felt small and stupid.

"For months, I barely spoke in public due to fear of rejection. I eventually taught myself to clearly annunciate all my words. I even studied the dictionary to make sure I knew what words meant. I subconsciously did everything I could to make sure that I would never be made to feel so stupid again."

Constantly Competing

Heidi continued: "At university, I used education to try to make me feel smart. Constantly competing, I always strived to be one of the best. But I never really believed I was clever. It was awful and it was exhausting. Even as an adult, I stayed for a decade in a banking job that I disliked because it gave me validation.

"At Healed for Life, the Holy Spirit brought me back to that childhood memory. I wept buckets as God healed my heart of the shame and pain buried deep within. It was like a massive weight lifted off my shoulders. Every sense of inadequacy was washed away.

"I have never encountered so much healing, confidence, transformation, joy and peace of mind in my entire life! Jesus completely transformed me. The change was noticed by my family, my friends and most of all by my husband. When the shame disappeared, I felt free to be me. Now I preach freely in front of big crowds without any insecurity."

Do You Deserve It?

I was working as a vice president in a public organization when I was approached to run a new unit at a leading company. Before I met the person who was offering me the job, my husband prepared me. He said, "Even if he offers you a major raise, don't look excited. Be calm and collected." I had lunch with the man. I distinctly remember that I ordered seafood spaghetti. There was a giant shrimp in the middle of the plate and its eyes looked straight at me. We chatted about the opportunity while we ate. Eventually, the gentleman got onto the subject of money. He offered me more than double my existing salary. When the perks and bonuses were included, it was nearly three times what I was earning! All I could hear were my husband's words so I stared at my spaghetti. I locked eyes with the shrimp in an attempt to avoid excitement. Its eyes looked like they were getting wider and wider! I managed to contain myself until lunch was finally over.

When my soon-to-be-boss was a block away, I called my husband and screamed with delight.

But that wasn't the end of it. Just as the company was putting the offer in writing, I received a phone call telling me that they were lowering the salary. It was a significant drop and it felt unpleasant. That weekend we had a prophet friend round for dinner. I shared the story with him, and he responded immediately. "You don't believe you're worth their original offer. Until you do, you won't get it."

I didn't like myself. In fact, I even felt like a fraud. I went into prayer and asked the Lord to reach into my heart and restore my self-worth. Within forty-eight hours, the original offer was back on the table. I worked there for two years and enjoyed great success. Let us look again at Proverbs 23.7: "As a man thinks in his heart, so he is". That means the image I have of myself will affect my life. Through my behavior, body language and conversation, I will project the value I place on myself. I wanted my salary to make me feel valuable. However, I had to begin the journey of discovering my worth before I could begin to expect a package I deserved.

Physical Features

The Shulamite, whose story is told in the Song of Songs, was possibly the most fortunate woman of her generation. She was married to a man who was extraordinarily wise, rich and powerful. King Solomon was also incredibly affectionate. He constantly spoke of his bride's breathtaking beauty. Despite his devotion, she still felt inferior. The Message version of Song of Songs 1:6 reveals her view of herself, "Don't look down on me because I'm dark, darkened by the sun's harsh rays. My brothers ridiculed me and sent me to work in the fields. They made me care for the face of the earth, but I had no time to care for my own face."

Privilege and promotion could not wash away the Shulamite's shame. We do not know exactly what went on with her brothers. We do know that their abusive behavior resulted in her face being badly burned. Years later, she still wore a veil and asked her husband to look away. Her facial scars marked her view of herself and made her feel self-conscious. She had to be healed in the loving arms of the king. My book *Lifting the Mask* uses her story to take readers on a healing journey.

If you feel ashamed about the way you look or speak, God wants to heal your heart. If you see yourself as stupid or small, the Holy Spirit wants to restore your view of yourself. He takes us back to the memories that marked us and tends our wounds. Romans 9:26 (NIV) explains, "In the very place where it was said to them, 'You are not my people,' there they will be called 'children of the living God.'" The Lord brings us back to the painful memory and then heals our hearts of all the hurt. He wipes away the shame and relieves the pain so that you are free to believe the truth. And the truth is that you are precious (Isaiah 43:4) and perfected in Him (Colossians 2:10). In 1 Corinthians 15:10, Paul the apostle made an amazing statement: "I am what I am by the favor of God." I pray that you will know that deep down. Let's pray:

Heavenly Father,

I realize that some of the experiences of my life have made me ashamed of the way I am. Some things that people said and did made me feel small and stupid. (Now tell the Lord about every painful memory that the Holy Spirit has brought to the surface. Speak to Him like you would a friend or close confidant. Jesus is the Wonderful Counselor. Tell Him what happened in as much detail as possible and explain how that made you feel.) I bring every hurt to You, Oh Lord. Thank

You that You are wiping away all my shame and reclothing me with dignity. I am grateful that You made me in Your image. I am what I am by the favor of God. I do not need to strive for success because I am complete in You.

I give You all the praise and glory.

In Jesus' name,

Amen.

Chapter 10

EMBARRASSMENT

When we are embarrassed, we become self-conscious. We can feel horribly awkward and out of place. It is a desperately unpleasant emotion that makes us want to hide or escape. All sorts of circumstances can be deeply embarrassing. Perhaps you were put down in public or ridiculed at work. Maybe you didn't get the message about the dress code for a function. You could have been the only one not to be invited to a big party or wedding and you only found out when you turned up. It could be that you were forced to reveal highly personal information in a public place. There are countless reasons why you might have been embarrassed.

Psalm 32:4b (NLT) expresses how it can affect us: "My strength evaporated like water in the summer heat." Exposure or ridicule can take away our vitality. However, once the moment has passed, we usually bury the memory as quickly as possible. Instead of facing the pain and being healed, we create defense mechanisms to ensure we don't get into that situation again.

Like A Fish Out Of Water

Some years ago, I accompanied a famous preacher on a ministry trip. This person does not like to travel alone, but the hosts of the conference had not provided an airline ticket for a companion. Hearing of her plight, my husband agreed to let me fly to the US to be with her on this trip. I planned my itinerary so that I would land in her home city and then travel with her to Pittsburgh. I did not want her to complete any part of the journey on her own. When I arrived, I discovered that the host church had in fact purchased a companion ticket for the preacher's assistant. I had traveled about 5,000 miles and incurred costs for absolutely no reason. I felt like a fool. I didn't know where to put myself. However, there was no going back so the three of us set off for Pennsylvania.

As we arrived at our hotel, I remember collapsing on the floor in my room in prayer. "Lord, I feel like a fool flying halfway across the world for no reason. I'm not needed, and I'm probably not wanted. I wish the ground would swallow me up!" I had not committed some iniquitous sin. I had not been publicly humiliated. Yet, I was unbearably ashamed. It is amazing how often shame pushes its way into our hearts. I poured out my pain in God's presence and He healed my heart. As a result, I was free to enjoy a hugely rewarding trip.

Awkward Moments

My husband and I traveled to South Africa for ministry. While we were there, we were invited by one of our host churches to a special celebration at a fancy restaurant. The young couple who delivered our invitation told us that the dress code was black tie formal wear. We had some formal clothes with us, so we managed to pull it off. As we walked into the function room, we quickly noticed that everyone else was in casual clothing. My husband was able to remove his jacket and bow tie, undo the top two buttons on his shirt and blend in. I was wearing a long black cocktail dress and silver stilettos. There was no way out of an evening of humiliation. Every conversation began with, "I know, I got the dress code wrong!"

If this had happened after my healing journey had begun, I would have handled the evening far better. I would probably have found it funny. However, at that stage in my life, even at the best of times, I felt insecure. I looked like a successful Christian woman. In reality, I was riddled with rejection. That night left me feeling ridiculous. I didn't do or say anything wrong, but I felt like a fool. I wanted to leave. Because that wasn't possible, I tried to hide. That is what shame does to its victims. It makes us want to cover ourselves with an invisible cloak.

Still Standing!

A famous preacher invited me to join her at an upper-class ladies' luncheon in London. The guests were all in top-notch designer dresses. Our sophisticated host showed us to our seats and the meeting began. About five minutes into a highly anointed message, this minister released the loudest and longest fart I have ever heard! If we had been in a down-to-earth setting, everybody would no doubt have burst out laughing. Not these ladies! Most pretended that they had not heard the extraordinary eruption. Thankfully, methane is invisible, but boy what a whiff!

The speaker turned crimson, made a funny comment, gathered herself together and then carried on. I was stunned. What would have reduced many ministers to a gibbering mess did not affect her. She probably had to deal with the embarrassment in prayer. However, she had been healed of the deep roots of shame and was therefore able to handle life's unexpected knocks.

Socially Awkward Situations

Socially awkward situations are far worse when we have hidden, unhealed hurts. When our hearts are really healed, we know our true value and we feel comfortable in our own skin. When we are genuinely secure, we don't worry what people think so public mistakes don't matter too much.

Being human means that we will slip up from time to time. It is a normal part of life. Occasionally, those slips will hurt. That is why we need to keep getting healed. However, if socially awkward experiences cause you to crumple, this is probably a sign that your heart needs healing. If you get unduly embarrassed when you make silly mistakes in public, these reactions are probably an indication that you have unresolved hurts. Of course, you need to be healed of the shame you feel in the moment. However, that is not the end of the story. Please ask the Lord to reveal the real issues deep down that make you susceptible to embarrassment. Get hold of my books. Lifting the Mask and My Whole Heart will help lead you on a healing journey. God wants us to be stable, secure and at peace in all circumstances.

Marital Status

Sometimes, even our status can make us feel awkward. Society seems to be set up for families. Churches can be the same. There are constant references to marriage, parenting, schooling, headship and so on. Most of us expect to get married. The vast majority of people desire to find that special someone and settle down. For some, that never happens. Instead, they may have learned to live alone - perhaps with the ache of loneliness. The pain does not always stop there. Isaiah 4:1 (Amplified) says, "And in that day seven women shall take hold of one man, saying, We will eat our own bread and provide our own apparel; only let us be called by your name to take away our reproach [of being unmarried]."

Of course, times have changed. However, I don't think the stigma of singleness has been dispelled completely. Perhaps you are alone, and you feel uncomfortable. You're always attending weddings by yourself. Friends who were once close drift away after they get married and spend time with couples instead. Your Heavenly Father wants to remove any reproach you feel as a result of your singleness. He wants you to know that you are the apple of His eye. The expression 'left on the shelf' is cruel and yet it accurately describes how some men and women feel. God wants to take away every ounce of stigma and show you the honor you deserve.

Stunted Growth

Another source of embarrassment can be slow progress. Perhaps you started a business and expected great success. However, trading is excruciatingly slow. Maybe you launched a ministry. God planted a picture of fruitfulness inside you and yet all you see is stagnation. Perhaps you know you are called to prosper, but you still live like a pauper. When our goals look like a pipe dream despite our dedication, it can make us feel stupid. We may try to hide the truth because it is embarrassing. No one tells their stories of mediocrity so all we hear from others is their resounding successes. Social media can magnify the problem because newsfeeds full of breakthroughs make us feel even more foolish.

You might be saying, "I should be enjoying my breakthrough by now. God promised it was coming soon!" The thing is that God has a different perspective to us. To Him, a thousand years are like a day. Even when Jesus was on earth, He told His followers, "...In a few days you will be baptized with the Holy Spirit." (Acts 1:5 NIV). In my opinion, a few means two or three. At most, it means five. In fact, the disciples had to wait six weeks for the outpouring of the Holy Spirit. A few days to Jesus was forty! Let's apply this to God's view of our progress. You may have been in business for many years, but the Lord might have been

THE MANY FACES OF SHAME

training you all this time for the breakthrough that is about to happen. Perhaps you have been waiting for what feels like an eternity for that promotion - not realizing that the new opportunity that is just around the corner is bigger than you ever imagined.

The Liar

Remember that the devil is constantly seeking to steal your promises. That is his mission (see John 10:10). He will use every available negative voice to try to make you give up on your dreams. Whispers in your ears may make you want to give up, but Jeremiah 7:4 says, "Do not trust in these lying words..." Most of the time, embarrassment is born out of self-consciousness. When we are over-sensitive, we worry that everyone else is thinking and talking about us. That is probably a lie. We have seen many men and women completely set free from self-consciousness at Healed for Life as God has gone to the root of the issue. As a result, embarrassment is no longer a major problem. If you know that you are over-sensitive or you get self-conscious, use Rebekah's Request to ask God to deal with the roots. Pray with me right now, "Father, if all is well, then why do I get embarrassed so easily? Shine Your light into my heart and reveal the root then heal me deep down, I pray, Oh Lord." Whatever memory the Lord brings to mind, share every detail in prayer and pour out your pain in His presence.

Embarrassment makes us want to crawl away or hide. If you feel like a fool in any area of your life, it's time to allow the Lord to take the shame away. Romans 8:14 says that, "The Sons of God are led by the Spirit of God." The problem with buried embarrassment is that it, rather than the Lord, can be leading us. We may avoid certain places or particular people. We could avoid eye contact or shy away from certain situations. The fear of being humiliated may be directing your decisions rather than the Holy Spirit. God wants to take away every ounce of embarrassment so that you can be free to follow God's wonderful plans for your life.

Overshadowed

One day as I was flicking through social media, I saw a photo of a friend. She was doing exactly what I had been believing God for years to achieve. Although I was genuinely delighted for her, I felt deeply discouraged. Her success made me doubt myself. I wondered why I was always falling short of my hopes and expectations. I got into the presence of God and started to pray, telling the Lord how I felt.

Almost immediately, I felt a check in my spirit. Like I said earlier, the devil often whispers untruths into our ears. He spins the stories of our circumstances to paint a gloomy picture. I was listening to the lies of the 'spin doctor'. The Holy Spirit reminded me that God shows no partiality (Acts 10:34). What He does for one, He will gladly do for another. The very picture that God showed me to encourage me the devil used to drag me down.

As I sat in God's presence, I apologized. I had allowed myself to be deceived by the devil and pushed into discouragement. I started to encourage myself instead. How do we do that? The Bible tells us that our tongues are like the rudders of a ship (James 3:4-5). You encourage yourself the same way you would encourage someone else. You remind yourself of the goodness and faithfulness of God. You rehearse His promises in your heart. When you tell yourself the truth instead of believing the enemy's lies, you will be strengthened.

Put-downs

A few years ago, I was at a big conference with an array of amazing ministers. I spotted one of them who I had met two years earlier. As the gentleman walked past, I said hello, reminding him of our meeting. He glanced at me with what looked like a mixture of disgust and disbelief. He shrugged his shoulders and moved on. In a matter of seconds, I was cut down to size.

Even though this was relatively insignificant, it hit me. I regretted reaching out and wanted to withdraw. The enemy exploits this type of experience. He will tell us to avoid any behavior that could produce the same outcome. I was tempted to change my normally friendly manner. This is one of the ways the enemy harms us in the long term. He causes us to step back, shut down and hide.

As soon as I felt these emotions rising within me, I pulled myself aside. I told God that this man's reaction had hurt me, and I asked Him to heal my heart. It was not long before an inner peace was restored. I then let go of the offence. The following day when this minister was due to speak, my heart was open, and I was expectant. I probably received more from his session than any other. The enemy's plan to rob my blessing had been thwarted.

Belittled

King David spoke of the shame of being belittled. In Psalms 69:20 (Amplified), he said, "Insults and reproach have broken my heart; I am full of heaviness and I am distressingly sick..." Reproach is that mixture of undermining words and a dismissive or mocking attitude. With one remark, we can be torn apart inside. Perhaps you have been slurred by your spouse, belittled by brothers or undermined at the office. Maybe you were publicly humiliated. Whatever happened, it can leave us feeling so small. Dishonor can be intensely uncomfortable. As a result, we often try to deny the way we are feeling. We think that if we ignore the inner churn, it will go away. We push it down, but we end up damaged by its effects.

The Way Out

If you have been embarrassed, God wants to heal your heart. If you have been disgraced, the Lord wants to restore your dignity. The first step is to acknowledge how uncomfortable the experience made you feel. Tell the Holy Spirit what you went through. Explain if you were squashed or humiliated. Be as real and specific as possible. Then ask your Heavenly Father to heal your heart.

The second step is to let go of any offence. The enemy wants you to hold resentment, but the Bible tells us that it is destructive. Forgive the person who humiliated you. Give them to God and let go of what they did. We never know why people do what they do so we cannot judge their actions. Give the incident and the person to God in prayer. I recommend you seal your restoration by asking God to bless any person who hurt you.

Scripture is clear. You and I can live free from shame. Romans 10:11 (NLT) says, "Anyone who trusts in Him will never be disgraced." When we take our eyes off people and live life to please God, there will be great protection from the power of shame. As you allow the Lord to deal with every deep root of shame on the inside, you will be able to enjoy a life free from humiliation and embarrassment. Let's pray.

Heavenly Father,

I realize that I have been carrying buried embarrassment in my heart. I have felt a fool as a result of my own actions, but also because of things that have been said and done. I ask You to heal my heart. (Now tell the Lord about the memories that He has brought back. Explain what happened and how it made you feel. Bring the embarrassment into the light of God's presence and tell your Heavenly Father all that happened.) I give you every awkward memory, Lord, and I ask You to heal my heart of every put-down and any public mistake I have made.

I choose today to forgive anyone who has humiliated me. Just as You forgive me of all my sins, so I forgive those who have harmed me. I forgive (Now say the names of those who have hurt you) for what they did to hurt me. I release them into Your hands. I let go of any offence that I was holding. Father, I let go completely and ask You to bless those who have wounded me.

Thank You, Lord, that I am fearfully and wonderfully made. Thank You that I am what I am by the favor of God (1 Corinthians 15:10). Thank You that I can enjoy my life, safe in the knowledge that You will never put me to shame. Embarrassment will no longer have a hold on my life. I let go and I trust You, Lord, to take care of me.

In Jesus' name, I pray,

Amen.

P.S. DO YOU FEEL LIKE A VICTIM?

A victim is a person who has suffered some sort of injury. Most people have been victims at one time or another. However, one of the enemy's tactics is to lead people into a victim mentality. If you have suffered a great deal at the hands of various people, you may end up believing that you have a target on your back. If you have gone through more than your fair share of pain and pressure, it can seem like life is against you. When we have a victim mentality, we end up negatively interpreting the circumstances around us. We feel like the world is a tough place and that life is harder for us than it is for others. This mentality can become a prison, locking us in with pain and hardship. Shame always tries to make people feel like victims, so it is important that we ask ourselves if this has affected our lives. A victim mentality almost always produces self-pity. When we eradicate self-pity, our victim mentality will crumble. We can arise knowing the truth, that we are victors.

Survivor

In the years after our daughter died, I saw myself as a survivor. I was someone who had been to hell and back and made it out alive. I believed that I deserved extra compassion because of the loss I had suffered. When times were tough, I expected special concessions. When life was good, I saw myself as a hero for being happy. Most of all, I saw myself as different. When we see ourselves as different, we make allowances for all sorts of things. We accept isolation, allow negative thinking and excuse bad behavior. When we believe our lives are unusual, we often think that we can't achieve the breakthroughs that others enjoy. Self-pity can leave us feeling cheated and dejected. It erodes our faith. It makes us feel like slowing down or giving up. Left unchecked, self-pity is a destiny-destroyer. It causes its victims to be preoccupied with themselves.

The Bible teaches that each one of us is unique. God has a tailored plan for your life that reflects your individual design. At the same time, one of the core lessons of Ecclesiastes is that nothing we go through is new: "That which has been is what will be, that which is done is what will be done, and there is nothing new under the sun. Is there anything of which it may be said, 'See, this is new'? It has already been in ancient times before us." (Ecclesiastes 1:9-10)

In truth, I was not that different from anyone else. History often repeats itself. Countless couples across the world have lost their children to an untimely death. Indeed, many have lost entire families. Scores of parents have suffered like me and come out strong from the experience. In the same way, others have endured battles that are similar to yours and emerged successfully on the other side. Every test or trial has been faced by others down through the centuries (1 Corinthians 10:13). When we realize that our struggle is not all that different from the battles that others have had to fight, it can help us to put our lives in some sort of perspective. If we take our eyes off our individual issues and instead look to the greatness of God, the Lord can start to work within.

Sad End

I find the final scenes of Prophet Elijah's life sad (see 1 Kings 19). After one of the most extraordinary victories on Mount

133

Carmel, defeating the prophets of Baal and proving the power of God, Elijah ran away, terrified of Jezebel. He escaped to a cave while displaying telltale signs of self-pity. When we feel sorry for ourselves, we often want to retreat and hide in a place where we can wallow in our circumstances. We believe the lie that our pain is unique or our circumstances are the worst. Elijah cried out to God that he was the only servant of His who was alive. Yet the Bible states that there were 7,000 men and women who maintained their faith in Yahweh. Believing that he alone was left, Elijah told the Lord that he wanted to die. Self-pity always tells us to give up. It was at this point in Elijah's life that God called time on this mighty man of God and raised up Elisha in his place.

If you have a victim mentality or if you have been feeling sorry for yourself, I encourage you to do two things. First of all, acknowledge deep down that you are not a victim and that you are not alone. Recognize right now that your troubles are common to man, as Scripture says. Others have fought the battles you are fighting and come out as conquerors. You can too. I encourage you to read my book Doorway to your Destiny, which has a whole chapter dedicated to breaking self-pity. Second, allow gratitude to rise up on the inside. Think of every good thing that God has done for you over the years and start to thank Him from the bottom of your heart. Gratitude is the greatest antidote to self-pity. Develop real, heartfelt gratitude. Lip service thank yous won't work. Let's pray.

Heavenly Father,

I realize that I have believed the lies of the enemy that I am a victim. I believed that my life was worse than the lives of others and that my suffering made me different. I break the power of every lie over my life, in Jesus' name. Thank

You that Your Word is true. There is nothing new under the sun. The kinds of tests and trials that I have gone through have affected many people across the world. I ask for Your forgiveness for feeling sorry for myself. You are a good Father and You have preserved me to this day. Thank You that You will heal every hurt that I surrender. Thank You that my life is turning around.

I declare that I am not a victim. Through Jesus, I am a victor (1 Corinthians 15:57). I break every mindset that made me believe that I was a victim. Thank You that I have access to every heavenly blessing through Jesus. Thank You that I am privileged to be Your child. Thank You for Your wonderful love and great kindness. I am grateful for every good and perfect gift that You have given me. I give You praise. You are a good, good Father and I am deeply grateful for all You have done and will do for me.

In Jesus' name, I pray,

Amen.

WHAT NEXT?

Your heart is probably your most valuable, and yet your most vulnerable, asset. This book is just part of your journey to wholeness and freedom. As you finish this book, make the decision to continue to prioritize your inner wellbeing. Visit our website JoNaughton.com to find out about our range of resources to help you to wholeness. We run half day, full day and two-day events. Above all, look after your heart every day of your life for it determines the course of your life.

"I am convinced and sure of this very thing, that He Who began a good work in you will continue until the day of Jesus Christ (right up to the time of His return), developing [that good work] and perfecting and binging it to full completion in you." (Philippians 1:6 AMP)

Let that word sink deep into you. God is preparing you for your destiny. He has already started the job and He will be faithful to finish it.

AN INVITATION

If you would like to ask Jesus to become the Lord of your life, I would be honored to lead you in a simple prayer. The Bible says that God loves you and that Jesus wants to draw close to you: "Behold I stand at the door and knock. If anyone hears My voice and opens the door, I will come in." (Revelation 3:20). If you would like to know Jesus as your Friend, your Savior and your Lord, the first step is to ask. Pray this prayer:

Dear Lord,

I know that You love me and have a wonderful plan for my life. I ask You to come into my heart today and be my Savior and Lord. Forgive me for all my sins, I pray. Thank You that because You died on the cross for me, I am forgiven of every wrong I have ever committed, and I am completely cleansed from my past. I give my life to You entirely and ask You to lead me in Your ways from now on. In Jesus' name, amen.

If you have prayed this prayer for the first time, it will be important to tell a Christian friend what you prayed and to find a good church. Just as a newborn baby needs nourishment and care, so you (and all Christians) need the support of other believers as you start your new life as a follower of Jesus Christ.

You can watch free Bible messages that will help to build your faith on Harvest Church London's YouTube channel. You can follow me on Twitter (@naughtonjo), go on Facebook and like my public page (Jo Naughton), subscribe to my YouTube channel (Jo Naughton) and follow me on Instagram (@naughtonjo). God bless you!

ABOUT THE AUTHOR

Jo Naughton is the founder of Healed for Life, a ministry dedicated to helping people be free to fulfill their God-given purpose. Together with her husband Paul, Jo pastors Harvest Church in London, England. A public relations executive turned pastor, Jo's previous career included working for Prince Charles as an executive VP of his largest charity. After reaching the pinnacle of the public relations world, Jo felt the call of God to full-time ministry. She is a regular guest on TV and radio shows in the US and UK.

An international speaker and author, Jo ministers with a heart-piercing anointing, sharing with great personal honesty in conferences and at churches around the world. Her passion is to see people set free from all inner hindrances so that they can fulfill their God-given destiny. Countless people have testified to having received powerful and life-changing healing through her ministry. Jo and Paul have two wonderful children, Ben and Abby.

You can connect with Jo via:
jonaughton.com
Facebook (public page - Jo Naughton)
Twitter (@naughtonjo)
Instagram (@naughtonjo)
For more information about Harvest Church London, visit
harvestchurch.org.uk

Also by the Author:

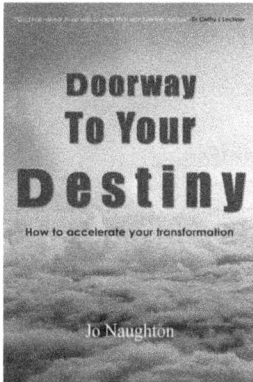

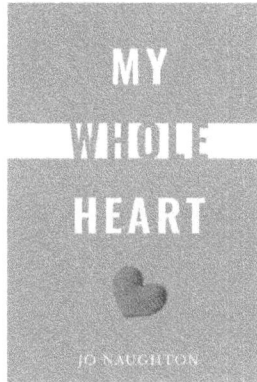

Lifting
THE MASK

WHO ARE YOU WHEN NO-ONE'S LOOKING?

Jo Naughton

Dreamstealers
How to stop your destiny being stolen

Jo Naughton

FOREWORD BY GUILLERMO MALDONADO

30-DAY
DETOX
FOR YOUR SOUL

JO NAUGHTON

Doorway
To Your
Destiny
How to accelerate your transformation

Jo Naughton

MY
WHOLE
HEART

JO NAUGHTON

All Jo Naughton's books are available at: jonaughton.com